RUNES FOR MINDFULNESS
DAILY PRACTICE JOURNAL

A DAILY JOURNAL FOR RUNE
PRACTICE, MINDFULNESS, AND
SELF-DISCOVERY

This journal belongs to

_____

Dear Pathfinder,

Thank you for choosing to walk this mindful path with me. This journal is a space for you to explore the world of runes through your own reflections, thoughts, and insights.

May it become both a mirror and a map. Helping you notice the patterns in your days, the lessons in each moment, and the quiet wisdom that's always been within you.

There is no single 'right' way to work with the runes. Let your intuition be your guide. Some days your writing will flow easily, other days you may simply jot a single thought and both are perfectly enough. What matters is showing up for yourself, with honesty and openness.

As you draw each rune and record its presence in your day, may you find clarity where there was confusion, stillness where there was noise, and courage where there was doubt. Let these ancient symbols be gentle reminders to pause, breathe, and reconnect with the present.

This is your journey now—unique, personal, and ever-evolving. I'm honoured to be a small part of it.

With warmth and gratitude,

Table of Contents

- How to Use This Journal

- Quick Rune Reference & Meditation Script Chart

- Daily Practice Pages

- Weekly Check-Ins

- Monthly Tracker Overview & Reflections

- Blank Rune Outlines

How to Use This Journal

This journal is your space to explore mindfulness through the wisdom of the Elder Futhark runes. It's designed to be flexible. You can use it daily, weekly, or whenever you feel called to connect with the runes. There's no "right" way, only the way that works for you.

Step 1 – Draw Your Rune
Begin your day (or session) by drawing a rune from your rune set, or simply choose one that resonates with you in the moment.

Step 2 – Record Your First Impressions
On your Daily Practice Page, jot down your thoughts, feelings, or any intuitive messages that arise when you see the rune. You can use the Quick Rune Meanings Chart as a guide, but also trust your own instincts.

Step 3 – Carry the Rune's Energy with You
Throughout the day, notice where the rune's message appears, whether in your thoughts, conversations, decisions, or unexpected moments.

Step 4 – Weekly Check-Ins
Use the Weekly Check-Ins to reflect on patterns, progress, and insights. This helps you deepen your connection to both mindfulness and the runes.

Step 5 – Monthly Overview & Tracker
The Monthly Overview & Tracker helps you see the bigger picture, spotting recurring runes, themes, or emotional shifts over time.

Step 6 – Reflect at the End
The Looking Back. Final Reflections section is where you can summarise your journey and the ways your understanding (and perhaps your life) has shifted.

Step 7 – Get Creative
The Blank Rune Outlines give you a place to draw, colour, or decorate runes as part of your mindfulness practice.

Remember: this is your personal journey. You can\ adapt the prompts, skip sections, or add your own creative touches. Let the runes be your companions in slowing down, noticing the present moment, and finding meaning in everyday life.

Quick Rune Reference & Meditation Script Chart

Symbol	Rune Name/Theme	Meditation Script:
Blank Rune	**ODIN'S RUNE** – The Sacred Unknown (aka Wyrd or Blank Rune) **Theme:** Trust, fate, divine will	Breathe into silence. No symbol appears, only space. This is Odin's Rune, the unknowable void. Ask: *Can I surrender to mystery? Am I willing to release the need for answers?* Sit in this sacred pause, no meaning to grasp, no sign to decipher. Just breathe. Just being. Here, anything is possible. You are ready.

Symbol	Rune/Theme	Meditation Script:
	FEHU - Abundance & Beginnings **Theme:** Prosperity, Possessions, New Beginnings	Find a comfortable seated position. Close your eyes gently. Breathe in deeply… and breathe out slowly. Bring your awareness to the energy stirring within you. Visualise the rune Fehu glowing softly in a golden hue. Let it represent abundance. Not just material wealth, but also love, experience, and opportunity. Repeat silently: *"I welcome prosperity. I honour what I have and what is yet to come."* Breathe in the possibility of new beginnings. With each breath, feel yourself grounded and open to growth. When you're ready, return your awareness to the present.
	URUZ - Strength & Vitality / **Theme:** Physical strength, resilience, health	Find stillness and let your breath become slow and steady. Visualise Uruz, shaped like the curved horns of ancient aurochs. Feel strength rising from deep within your bones, muscles, and will. Repeat silently: *"I embody strength. I am resilient. I am alive."* Let this energy fill you. Sit with it and honour your body. Return to the present with gratitude.
	THURISAZ – Boundaries & Protection **Theme:** Defence, powerful transformation, warning	Draw a breath in through your nose… and out through your mouth. Visualise Thurisaz, bright and bold like a lightning bolt. Feel its protective shield forming around you. Reflect on where you need boundaries in your life. Repeat silently: *"I protect my space. I honour my strength. I am ready for transformation."* Anchor this intention with your breath. Remain here until you feel steady.
	ANSUZ – Wisdom & Communication **Theme:** Divine message, expression, inspiration	Relax your shoulders. Visualise Ansuz, the rune of divine breath and inspired speech. Imagine wind moving through trees, whispers of ancient knowledge. Repeat silently: *"I speak truth. I listen deeply. I am guided by wisdom."* Stay here. Listen. Receive. Feel your throat and heart gently align. Carry this awareness into your day.

Symbol	Rune/Theme	Meditation Script:
ᚱ	**RAIDHO** – Journey and Rhythm **Theme:** Travel, life path, cosmic order	Settle in and tune to the rhythm of your breath. Inhaling… exhaling. Visualise Raidho, a wheel turning with purpose. See your path unfolding before you, one step at a time. Repeat silently: *"I trust the journey. I walk with purpose and flow."* Let this rhythm move through you. Return when you're ready, steady and sure.
ᚲ	**KENAZ** – Illumination and Creativity **Theme:** Torch, inner light, clarity	Take a breath. Visualise Kenaz, a flame in the darkness. Let it represent your insight and creative spark. Repeat silently: *"My light reveals. I see. I create."* Let this flame burn away confusion. Stay with the warmth and clarity it brings. Return carrying this light with you.
ᚷ	**GEBO** – Gift and Connection **Theme:** Generosity, balance, partnership	Breathe in deeply. Visualise the X-shape of Gebo. See it as a meeting point. Giving and receiving. Repeat silently: *"I give with grace. I receive with gratitude. I am connected."* Open your heart to reciprocity. Feel the strength in shared energy. Bring this harmony into your awareness.
ᚹ	**WUNJO** – Joy and Harmony **Theme:** Bliss, comfort, shared happiness	Smile softly. Deepen your breath. Visualise Wunjo, a flag of joy waving freely. Feel warmth spread through your chest. Repeat silently: *"Joy is within me. I invite harmony. I share happiness."* Feel light and uplifted. Return with this brightness held gently inside you.

Symbol	Rune Name/ Theme	Meditation Script:
ᚺ	**HAGALAZ** – Embracing the Storm **Theme:** Disruption, transformation, necessary change	Find stillness. Settle into your breath. Inhale deeply… exhale slowly. Visualise a storm gathering Not to fear, but to respect. See Hagalaz appear like hail, sudden and sharp. This rune reminds you that upheaval is a doorway to growth. Ask yourself: *What storm am I resisting? What must break for new patterns to emerge?* Let Hagalaz clear your fears. Feel tension release. This is not destruction without purpose—it's shaking loose what no longer serves you. Breathe out doubt. Breathe in strength. You stand in the eye of your own transformation.
ᚾ	**NAUTHIZ** – Necessity and Endurance **Theme:** Need, resistance, discipline	Breathe in slowly. Hold. Exhale gently. Visualise Nauthiz, a symbol of challenge and friction. Discomfort may rise; that's okay. Ask: *What do I truly need? Where am I called to endure?* Nauthiz offers growth through persistence. Sit with the tension and let it soften as you breathe. Choose patience and grace with each breath. Know your strength is being tempered for the path ahead.
ᛁ	**ISA** – Stillness and Focus **Theme:** Ice, stillness, clarity	Close your eyes and breathe deeply. Visualise a still, frozen lake, clear, silent, pure. See Isa suspended in ice, simple, straight, steady. Let its stillness calm your mind. Allow thoughts to settle like snowflakes on ice. Repeat silently: *"In stillness, I find clarity. I am centred. I am calm."* Stay with the quiet. There's no need to rush. Carry this stillness into your day.
ᛃ	**JERA** – Cycles of Completion **Theme:** Harvest, reward, natural cycles	Slow your breath. Tune into your body's rhythm. Visualise Jera glowing, a symbol of patient reward. Ask: *What am I growing? What stage am I in? Planting, nurturing, harvesting?* There is no rushing Jera. Trust the cycle. Breathe in this knowing. Celebrate what is complete. Make peace with what is yet to come. Let this rune ground you in natural timing.

Symbol	Rune Name/ Theme	Meditation Script:
	EIHWAZ – Strength of the Yew **Theme:** Defence, transformation, resilience	Let your breath root you, inhale through your nose, exhale through your mouth. Visualise Eihwaz, tall and protective like the ancient yew tree. Ask: *What am I being asked to face? Where must I hold my ground?* Feel resilience fortify your spine, rooted deep and reaching high. With each breath, know you are protected. You are both shield and seeker.
	PERTHRO – Mystery and Destiny **Theme:** Fate, secrets, chance	Breathe into the unknown. Release control. Visualise Perthro, a cup ready to be cast, its outcome unseen. Ask: *What mystery is unfolding? Can I surrender to not knowing?* Embrace the gamble, trust life's roll of the dice. Inhale curiosity. Exhale control. Let the mystery deepen your awareness. There is magic in uncertainty.
	ALGIZ – Sacred Protection **Theme:** Defence, boundaries, divine connection	Close your eyes and take a breath. Visualise a great antlered guardian rising before you, Algiz, sacred protection. Ask: *Where do I need shielding? What boundary must strengthen?* Feel its protective aura surrounding you. Its energy is fierce yet gentle, preserving what matters. With each breath, feel empowered. You are safe, supported, connected to something greater.
	SOWILO – The Inner Sun **Theme:** Victory, clarity, illumination	Breathe in sunlight. Let it fill your chest. Visualise Sowilo rising like the morning sun, warmth cutting through confusion. Ask: *Where do I need clarity? What part of me is ready to shine?* Let go of darkness with each breath. Let your inner sun rise. You are radiant, enough, moving forward.

Symbol	Rune Name/ Theme	Meditation Script:
↑	**TIWAZ** – The Courage to Act **Theme:** Honour, justice, self-sacrifice	Inhale courage. Exhale truth. Visualise Tiwaz, the upright spear of the warrior's rune. Ask: *Where must I take a stand? What value will I uphold at any cost?* Honour is not always easy but always right. Feel your resolve anchor here. Stand tall. Speak with integrity. Call forth your inner warrior of purpose.
ᛒ	**BERKANO** – Gentle Growth **Theme:** Nurture, birth, healing	Breathe gently, like a seedling stretching toward light. Visualise Berkano, the birch rune, soft and maternal. Ask: *What needs nurturing? Where can I show compassion to myself?* Let Berkano wrap around your heart like warm earth around roots. You are growing. Healing is happening, even if unseen. Each breath is an act of self-care. You are enough.
ᛖ	**EHWAZ** – Moving Forward Together **Theme:** Partnership, movement, progress	Inhale trust. Exhale fear. Visualise Ehwaz, two horses side by side, a symbol of partnership. Ask: *Where am I called to move forward? Who walks beside me?* Progress need not be lonely. With each breath, match your pace to your purpose. Together, you can move toward what's next.
ᛗ	**MANNAZ** – Knowing the Self **Theme:** Humanity, community, higher mind	Close your eyes and return to your breath. Inhale identity. Exhale illusion. Visualise Mannaz, the open, symmetrical human rune. Ask: *Who am I becoming? How do I connect as my true self?* Look inward and outward with care. You are part of a larger pattern. Your truth matters. Align with your highest self with each breath.

Symbol	Rune Name/ Theme	Meditation Script:
	LAGUZ – Flow and Intuition **Theme:** Water, emotion, inner knowing	Float into stillness. Breathe in... breathe out. Visualise Laguz rippling like water flowing through you. Ask: *Where am I resisting flow? What truths lie beneath the surface?* Trust your emotions. Dive deeper. Feel your breath like waves, steady, fluid, unforced. Let go. Trust the current. You are carried.
	INGWAZ – Sacred Space Within **Theme:** Fertility, rest, potential	Inhale deeply. Settle into quiet. Visualise Ingwaz, a sacred seed enclosed and whole. Ask: *What is gestating within me? What dream needs space and patience?* Not all progress is visible. Some growth happens in silence and dark. Honor your incubation with every breath. You are becoming.
	OTHALA – Legacy and Belonging **Theme:** Inheritance, ancestry, home	Breathe deeply. Feel the roots beneath your feet. Visualise Othala, ancient stone, firm and enduring. Ask: *What legacy do I carry? Where do I truly belong?* Connect with lineage, history, and chosen family. Let Othala anchor you in place and purpose. Each breath brings you home to yourself.
	DAGAZ – The Moment of Awakening **Theme:** Breakthrough, new beginnings, enlightenment	Breathe in the dawn. Exhale the night. Visualise Dagaz glowing on the horizon, the threshold of dark and light. Ask: *What awakening is ready to break through? Where is light returning?* This rune is hope and joy. Feel your consciousness expand with every breath. Step into the new. Let it begin.

Daily Practice Pages

GOOD MORNING

DAY & DATE: _____

Today's Rune

WHAT GUIDANCE IS THIS RUNE GIVING ME TODAY?

_____
_____
_____
_____
_____
_____

HOW IM FEELI ABOUT THIS D
- ☐ Happy
- ☐ Joyful
- ☐ Positive
- ☐ Energised
- ☐ Sad
- ☐ Angry
- ☐ Anguish
- ☐ Unhappy

TODAY GRATEFUL FOR:

1. _____
2. _____
3. _____

MY FOCUS FOR TODAY:

_____
_____
_____

How can today's rune help me make the most of today

GOOD EVENING

WHAT FELT IN HARMONY TODAY?

_____
_____
_____

WHAT FELT OUT OF BALANCE TODAY?

_____
_____
_____

WAS MY ENER WELL SPENT TODAY?
- ☐ Unfocused
- ☐ Distracted
- ☐ Steady
- ☐ Motivated
- ☐ Fully Engag

HOW DID THE ENERGY OR MEANING OF TODAY'S RUNE REVEAL ITSE

_____
_____

What small action I can take tomorrow to support m wellbeing...

GOOD MORNING DAY & DATE: _____

WHAT GUIDANCE IS THIS RUNE GIVING ME TODAY?

_____
_____
_____
_____
_____

Today's Rune

HOW IM FEELING ABOUT THIS DRAW?
☐ Happy
☐ Joyful
☐ Positive
☐ Energised
☐ Sad
☐ Angry
☐ Anguish
☐ Unhappy

TODAY GRATEFUL FOR:

_____
_____
_____

MY FOCUS FOR TODAY:

_____
_____
_____

How can today's rune help me make the most of today?

GOOD EVENING

WHAT FELT IN HARMONY TODAY?

_____
_____
_____

WHAT FELT OUT OF BALANCE TODAY?

_____
_____
_____

WAS MY ENERGY WELL SPENT TODAY?
☐ Unfocused
☐ Distracted
☐ Steady
☐ Motivated
☐ Fully Engaged

HOW DID THE ENERGY OR MEANING OF TODAY'S RUNE REVEAL ITSELF?

_____
_____

What small action I can take tomorrow to support my wellbeing…

GOOD MORNING

DAY & DATE: _____

Today's Rune

WHAT GUIDANCE IS THIS RUNE GIVING ME TODAY?
_____
_____
_____
_____
_____

HOW IM FEELI[NG] ABOUT THIS DR[AW]
☐ Happy
☐ Joyful
☐ Positive
☐ Energised
☐ Sad
☐ Angry
☐ Anguish
☐ Unhappy

TODAY GRATEFUL FOR:
1. _____
2. _____
3. _____

MY FOCUS FOR TODAY:
_____
_____
_____

How can today's rune help me make the most of today

GOOD EVENING

WHAT FELT IN HARMONY TODAY?
_____
_____
_____

WHAT FELT OUT OF BALANCE TODAY?
_____
_____
_____

WAS MY ENER[GY] WELL SPENT TODAY?
☐ Unfocused
☐ Distracted
☐ Steady
☐ Motivated
☐ Fully Engage[d]

HOW DID THE ENERGY OR MEANING OF TODAY'S RUNE REVEAL ITSE[LF]
_____
_____

What small action I can take tomorrow to support m[y] wellbeing…

OD MORNING

DAY & DATE: _____

Today's Rune

WHAT GUIDANCE IS THIS RUNE GIVING ME TODAY?

_____
_____
_____
_____

HOW IM FEELING ABOUT THIS DRAW?
- ☐ Happy
- ☐ Joyful
- ☐ Positive
- ☐ Energised
- ☐ Sad
- ☐ Angry
- ☐ Anguish
- ☐ Unhappy

DAY GRATEFUL FOR:

_____
_____
_____

MY FOCUS FOR TODAY:

_____
_____
_____

How can today's rune help me make the most of today?

_____

OD EVENING

HAT FELT IN HARMONY TODAY?

_____
_____
_____

HAT FELT OUT OF BALANCE TODAY?

_____
_____
_____

WAS MY ENERGY WELL SPENT TODAY?
- ☐ Unfocused
- ☐ Distracted
- ☐ Steady
- ☐ Motivated
- ☐ Fully Engaged

W DID THE ENERGY OR MEANING OF TODAY'S RUNE REVEAL ITSELF?

_____
_____

hat small action I can take tomorrow to support my ellbeing…

GOOD MORNING

DAY & DATE: ....

Today's Rune

WHAT GUIDANCE IS THIS RUNE GIVING ME TODAY?

_____
_____
_____
_____
_____

HOW IM FEELI[NG] ABOUT THIS D[AY]

- ☐ Happy
- ☐ Joyful
- ☐ Positive
- ☐ Energise[d]
- ☐ Sad
- ☐ Angry
- ☐ Anguish
- ☐ Unhappy

TODAY GRATEFUL FOR:

1. _____
2. _____
3. _____

MY FOCUS FOR TODAY:

_____
_____
_____

How can today's rune help me make the most of today

GOOD EVENING

WHAT FELT IN HARMONY TODAY?

_____
_____
_____

WHAT FELT OUT OF BALANCE TODAY?

_____
_____
_____

WAS MY ENER[GY] WELL SPEN[T] TODAY?

- ☐ Unfocused
- ☐ Distracted
- ☐ Steady
- ☐ Motivated
- ☐ Fully Engag[ed]

HOW DID THE ENERGY OR MEANING OF TODAY'S RUNE REVEAL ITSE[LF]

_____
_____

What small action I can take tomorrow to support m[y] wellbeing…

GOOD MORNING

DAY & DATE: _____

Today's Rune

WHAT GUIDANCE IS THIS RUNE GIVING ME TODAY?

_____
_____
_____
_____

HOW IM FEELING ABOUT THIS DRAW?

☐ Happy
☐ Joyful
☐ Positive
☐ Energised
☐ Sad
☐ Angry
☐ Anguish
☐ Unhappy

TODAY GRATEFUL FOR:

_____
_____
_____

MY FOCUS FOR TODAY:

_____
_____
_____

How can today's rune help me make the most of today?

_____

GOOD EVENING

WHAT FELT IN HARMONY TODAY?

_____
_____
_____

WHAT FELT OUT OF BALANCE TODAY?

_____
_____
_____

WAS MY ENERGY WELL SPENT TODAY?

☐ Unfocused
☐ Distracted
☐ Steady
☐ Motivated
☐ Fully Engaged

HOW DID THE ENERGY OR MEANING OF TODAY'S RUNE REVEAL ITSELF?

_____
_____

What small action I can take tomorrow to support my wellbeing...

GOOD MORNING   DAY & DATE: _____

WHAT GUIDANCE IS THIS RUNE GIVING ME TODAY?

_____
_____
_____
_____
_____

Today's Rune

HOW IM FEELI ABOUT THIS D
- ☐ Happy
- ☐ Joyful
- ☐ Positive
- ☐ Energised
- ☐ Sad
- ☐ Angry
- ☐ Anguish
- ☐ Unhappy

TODAY GRATEFUL FOR:
1. _____
2. _____
3. _____

MY FOCUS FOR TODAY:
_____
_____
_____

How can today's rune help me make the most of today

GOOD EVENING

WHAT FELT IN HARMONY TODAY?
_____
_____
_____

WHAT FELT OUT OF BALANCE TODAY?
_____
_____
_____

WAS MY ENER WELL SPEN TODAY?
- ☐ Unfocused
- ☐ Distracted
- ☐ Steady
- ☐ Motivated
- ☐ Fully Engag

HOW DID THE ENERGY OR MEANING OF TODAY'S RUNE REVEAL ITSE
_____
_____

What small action I can take tomorrow to support m wellbeing...

> "You can't stop the waves, but you can learn to surf."

Jon Kabat-Zinn

GOOD MORNING

DAY & DATE: _____

Today's Rune

WHAT GUIDANCE IS THIS RUNE GIVING ME TODAY?

_____
_____
_____
_____
_____

HOW IM FEELING ABOUT THIS DR
- ☐ Happy
- ☐ Joyful
- ☐ Positive
- ☐ Energised
- ☐ Sad
- ☐ Angry
- ☐ Anguish
- ☐ Unhappy

TODAY GRATEFUL FOR:
1. _____
2. _____
3. _____

MY FOCUS FOR TODAY:
_____
_____
_____

How can today's rune help me make the most of today

GOOD EVENING

WHAT FELT IN HARMONY TODAY?
_____
_____
_____

WHAT FELT OUT OF BALANCE TODAY?
_____
_____
_____

WAS MY ENERGY WELL SPENT TODAY?
- ☐ Unfocused
- ☐ Distracted
- ☐ Steady
- ☐ Motivated
- ☐ Fully Engaged

HOW DID THE ENERGY OR MEANING OF TODAY'S RUNE REVEAL ITSELF
_____
_____

What small action I can take tomorrow to support my wellbeing…

OD MORNING   DAY & DATE: ....

WHAT GUIDANCE IS THIS RUNE GIVING ME TODAY?

_____
_____
_____
_____

Today's Rune

HOW IM FEELING ABOUT THIS DRAW?

☐ Happy
☐ Joyful
☐ Positive
☐ Energised
☐ Sad
☐ Angry
☐ Anguish
☐ Unhappy

DAY GRATEFUL FOR:

_____
_____
_____

MY FOCUS FOR TODAY:

_____
_____
_____

How can today's rune help me make the most of today?

OD EVENING

HAT FELT IN HARMONY TODAY?

_____
_____
_____

HAT FELT OUT OF BALANCE TODAY?

_____
_____

WAS MY ENERGY WELL SPENT TODAY?

☐ Unfocused
☐ Distracted
☐ Steady
☐ Motivated
☐ Fully Engaged

W DID THE ENERGY OR MEANING OF TODAY'S RUNE REVEAL ITSELF?

_____
_____

What small action I can take tomorrow to support my ellbeing…

GOOD MORNING   DAY & DATE: _____

Today's Rune

WHAT GUIDANCE IS THIS RUNE GIVING ME TODAY?
_____
_____
_____
_____
_____

HOW IM FEELING ABOUT THIS DAY
☐ Happy
☐ Joyful
☐ Positive
☐ Energised
☐ Sad
☐ Angry
☐ Anguish
☐ Unhappy

TODAY GRATEFUL FOR:

1. _____
2. _____
3. _____

MY FOCUS FOR TODAY:
_____
_____
_____

How can today's rune help me make the most of today

GOOD EVENING

WHAT FELT IN HARMONY TODAY?
_____
_____
_____

WHAT FELT OUT OF BALANCE TODAY?
_____
_____
_____

WAS MY ENERGY WELL SPENT TODAY?
☐ Unfocused
☐ Distracted
☐ Steady
☐ Motivated
☐ Fully Engaged

HOW DID THE ENERGY OR MEANING OF TODAY'S RUNE REVEAL ITSELF
_____
_____

What small action I can take tomorrow to support my wellbeing…

GOOD MORNING

DAY & DATE: ....

WHAT GUIDANCE IS THIS RUNE GIVING ME TODAY?

_____

_____

_____

_____

_____

Today's Rune

HOW IM FEELING ABOUT THIS DRAW?

☐ Happy
☐ Joyful
☐ Positive
☐ Energised
☐ Sad
☐ Angry
☐ Anguish
☐ Unhappy

TODAY GRATEFUL FOR:

_____

_____

_____

MY FOCUS FOR TODAY:

_____

_____

_____

How can today's rune help me make the most of today?

GOOD EVENING

WHAT FELT IN HARMONY TODAY?

_____

_____

_____

WHAT FELT OUT OF BALANCE TODAY?

_____

_____

_____

WAS MY ENERGY WELL SPENT TODAY?

☐ Unfocused
☐ Distracted
☐ Steady
☐ Motivated
☐ Fully Engaged

HOW DID THE ENERGY OR MEANING OF TODAY'S RUNE REVEAL ITSELF?

_____

_____

What small action I can take tomorrow to support my wellbeing…

GOOD MORNING

DAY & DATE: ....

Today's Rune

WHAT GUIDANCE IS THIS RUNE GIVING ME TODAY?

_____
_____
_____
_____
_____

HOW IM FEELI ABOUT THIS D

- ☐ Happy
- ☐ Joyful
- ☐ Positive
- ☐ Energised
- ☐ Sad
- ☐ Angry
- ☐ Anguish
- ☐ Unhappy

TODAY GRATEFUL FOR:

1. _____
2. _____
3. _____

MY FOCUS FOR TODAY:

_____
_____
_____

How can today's rune help me make the most of today

GOOD EVENING

WHAT FELT IN HARMONY TODAY?

_____
_____
_____

WHAT FELT OUT OF BALANCE TODAY?

_____
_____
_____

WAS MY ENER WELL SPEN TODAY?

- ☐ Unfocused
- ☐ Distracted
- ☐ Steady
- ☐ Motivated
- ☐ Fully Engag

HOW DID THE ENERGY OR MEANING OF TODAY'S RUNE REVEAL ITSE

_____
_____

What small action I can take tomorrow to support m wellbeing…

GOOD MORNING

DAY & DATE: _____

WHAT GUIDANCE IS THIS RUNE GIVING ME TODAY?

_____

_____

_____

_____

Today's Rune

HOW IM FEELING ABOUT THIS DRAW?
☐ Happy
☐ Joyful
☐ Positive
☐ Energised
☐ Sad
☐ Angry
☐ Anguish
☐ Unhappy

TODAY GRATEFUL FOR:

_____

_____

_____

MY FOCUS FOR TODAY:

_____

_____

_____

How can today's rune help me make the most of today?

GOOD EVENING

WHAT FELT IN HARMONY TODAY?

_____

_____

_____

WHAT FELT OUT OF BALANCE TODAY?

_____

_____

_____

WAS MY ENERGY WELL SPENT TODAY?
☐ Unfocused
☐ Distracted
☐ Steady
☐ Motivated
☐ Fully Engaged

HOW DID THE ENERGY OR MEANING OF TODAY'S RUNE REVEAL ITSELF?

_____

_____

What small action I can take tomorrow to support my wellbeing…

GOOD MORNING

DAY & DATE: ....

Today's Rune

WHAT GUIDANCE IS THIS RUNE GIVING ME TODAY?

_____
_____
_____
_____
_____

HOW IM FEELI ABOUT THIS DR
- ☐ Happy
- ☐ Joyful
- ☐ Positive
- ☐ Energised
- ☐ Sad
- ☐ Angry
- ☐ Anguish
- ☐ Unhappy

TODAY GRATEFUL FOR:

1. _____
2. _____
3. _____

MY FOCUS FOR TODAY:

_____
_____
_____

How can today's rune help me make the most of today

GOOD EVENING

WHAT FELT IN HARMONY TODAY?

_____
_____
_____

WHAT FELT OUT OF BALANCE TODAY?

_____
_____

WAS MY ENER WELL SPENT TODAY?
- ☐ Unfocused
- ☐ Distracted
- ☐ Steady
- ☐ Motivated
- ☐ Fully Engag

HOW DID THE ENERGY OR MEANING OF TODAY'S RUNE REVEAL ITSE

_____
_____

What small action I can take tomorrow to support m wellbeing…

"A WISE PERSON'S WEALTH IS IN THEIR WORDS."

Adapted from the Hávamál

GOOD MORNING

DAY & DATE: _____

Today's Rune

WHAT GUIDANCE IS THIS RUNE GIVING ME TODAY?

_____
_____
_____
_____

HOW IM FEELING ABOUT THIS D

- ☐ Happy
- ☐ Joyful
- ☐ Positive
- ☐ Energised
- ☐ Sad
- ☐ Angry
- ☐ Anguish
- ☐ Unhappy

TODAY GRATEFUL FOR:

1. _____
2. _____
3. _____

MY FOCUS FOR TODAY:

_____
_____
_____

How can today's rune help me make the most of today

GOOD EVENING

WHAT FELT IN HARMONY TODAY?

_____
_____
_____

WHAT FELT OUT OF BALANCE TODAY?

_____
_____
_____

WAS MY ENERGY WELL SPENT TODAY?

- ☐ Unfocused
- ☐ Distracted
- ☐ Steady
- ☐ Motivated
- ☐ Fully Engaged

HOW DID THE ENERGY OR MEANING OF TODAY'S RUNE REVEAL ITSELF

_____
_____

What small action I can take tomorrow to support my wellbeing...

GOOD MORNING

DAY & DATE: ....

Today's Rune

WHAT GUIDANCE IS THIS RUNE GIVING ME TODAY?

_____
_____
_____
_____

HOW IM FEELING ABOUT THIS DRAW?

☐ Happy
☐ Joyful
☐ Positive
☐ Energised
☐ Sad
☐ Angry
☐ Anguish
☐ Unhappy

TODAY GRATEFUL FOR:

_____
_____
_____

MY FOCUS FOR TODAY:

_____
_____
_____

How can today's rune help me make the most of today?

GOOD EVENING

WHAT FELT IN HARMONY TODAY?

_____
_____
_____

WHAT FELT OUT OF BALANCE TODAY?

_____
_____
_____

WAS MY ENERGY WELL SPENT TODAY?

☐ Unfocused
☐ Distracted
☐ Steady
☐ Motivated
☐ Fully Engaged

HOW DID THE ENERGY OR MEANING OF TODAY'S RUNE REVEAL ITSELF?

_____
_____

What small action I can take tomorrow to support my wellbeing...

GOOD MORNING

DAY & DATE: ....

Today's Rune

WHAT GUIDANCE IS THIS RUNE GIVING ME TODAY?

_____
_____
_____
_____
_____

HOW IM FEELING ABOUT THIS DAY

☐ Happy
☐ Joyful
☐ Positive
☐ Energised
☐ Sad
☐ Angry
☐ Anguish
☐ Unhappy

TODAY GRATEFUL FOR:

1. _____
2. _____
3. _____

MY FOCUS FOR TODAY:

_____
_____
_____

How can today's rune help me make the most of today

GOOD EVENING

WHAT FELT IN HARMONY TODAY?

_____
_____
_____

WHAT FELT OUT OF BALANCE TODAY?

_____
_____
_____

WAS MY ENERGY WELL SPENT TODAY?

☐ Unfocused
☐ Distracted
☐ Steady
☐ Motivated
☐ Fully Engaged

HOW DID THE ENERGY OR MEANING OF TODAY'S RUNE REVEAL ITSELF

_____
_____

What small action I can take tomorrow to support my wellbeing...

GOOD MORNING

DAY & DATE: ....

Today's Rune

WHAT GUIDANCE IS THIS RUNE GIVING ME TODAY?

_____

_____

_____

_____

HOW IM FEELING ABOUT THIS DRAW?

☐ Happy
☐ Joyful
☐ Positive
☐ Energised
☐ Sad
☐ Angry
☐ Anguish
☐ Unhappy

TODAY GRATEFUL FOR:

_____

_____

_____

MY FOCUS FOR TODAY:

_____

_____

_____

> How can today's rune help me make the most of today?

GOOD EVENING

WHAT FELT IN HARMONY TODAY?

_____

_____

_____

WHAT FELT OUT OF BALANCE TODAY?

_____

_____

_____

WAS MY ENERGY WELL SPENT TODAY?

☐ Unfocused
☐ Distracted
☐ Steady
☐ Motivated
☐ Fully Engaged

HOW DID THE ENERGY OR MEANING OF TODAY'S RUNE REVEAL ITSELF?

_____

_____

> What small action I can take tomorrow to support my wellbeing…

GOOD MORNING

DAY & DATE: _____

Today's Rune

WHAT GUIDANCE IS THIS RUNE GIVING ME TODAY?
_____
_____
_____
_____
_____
_____

HOW IM FEELING ABOUT THIS DRAW
- ☐ Happy
- ☐ Joyful
- ☐ Positive
- ☐ Energised
- ☐ Sad
- ☐ Angry
- ☐ Anguish
- ☐ Unhappy

TODAY GRATEFUL FOR:
1. _____
2. _____
3. _____

MY FOCUS FOR TODAY:
_____
_____
_____

How can today's rune help me make the most of today

GOOD EVENING

WHAT FELT IN HARMONY TODAY?
_____
_____
_____

WHAT FELT OUT OF BALANCE TODAY?
_____
_____
_____

WAS MY ENERGY WELL SPENT TODAY?
- ☐ Unfocused
- ☐ Distracted
- ☐ Steady
- ☐ Motivated
- ☐ Fully Engaged

HOW DID THE ENERGY OR MEANING OF TODAY'S RUNE REVEAL ITSELF
_____
_____

What small action I can take tomorrow to support my wellbeing…

OD MORNING DAY & DATE: _____

WHAT GUIDANCE IS THIS RUNE
GIVING ME TODAY?

_____
_____
_____
_____

Today's Rune

HOW IM FEELING
ABOUT THIS DRAW?
☐ Happy
☐ Joyful
☐ Positive
☐ Energised
☐ Sad
☐ Angry
☐ Anguish
☐ Unhappy

DAY GRATEFUL FOR:

_____
_____
_____

MY FOCUS FOR TODAY:

_____
_____
_____

How can today's rune help me make the most of today?

OD EVENING

AT FELT IN HARMONY TODAY?

_____
_____
_____

AT FELT OUT OF BALANCE TODAY?

_____
_____
_____
_____

WAS MY ENERGY
WELL SPENT
TODAY?

☐ Unfocused
☐ Distracted
☐ Steady
☐ Motivated
☐ Fully Engaged

W DID THE ENERGY OR MEANING OF TODAY'S RUNE REVEAL ITSELF?

_____
_____

What small action I can take tomorrow to support my ellbeing…

GOOD MORNING

DAY & DATE: ....

Today's Rune

WHAT GUIDANCE IS THIS RUNE GIVING ME TODAY?

_____
_____
_____
_____
_____
_____

HOW IM FEELI ABOUT THIS D
- ☐ Happy
- ☐ Joyful
- ☐ Positive
- ☐ Energise
- ☐ Sad
- ☐ Angry
- ☐ Anguish
- ☐ Unhappy

TODAY GRATEFUL FOR:

1. _____
2. _____
3. _____

MY FOCUS FOR TODAY:

_____
_____
_____

How can today's rune help me make the most of today

GOOD EVENING

WHAT FELT IN HARMONY TODAY?

_____
_____
_____

WHAT FELT OUT OF BALANCE TODAY?

_____
_____
_____

WAS MY ENER WELL SPEN TODAY?
- ☐ Unfocused
- ☐ Distracted
- ☐ Steady
- ☐ Motivated
- ☐ Fully Engag

HOW DID THE ENERGY OR MEANING OF TODAY'S RUNE REVEAL ITSE

_____
_____

What small action I can take tomorrow to support m wellbeing...

Story time

The Stag and the Thistle

In the misty highlands, where the morning dew clings to heather and the wind carries the scent of rain, a proud stag wandered. His antlers reached skyward like branches of an ancient tree, and his step was strong.

He searched for the sweetest grass in the valley — soft, tender, and plentiful. Yet, on a rocky slope where little else grew, he found a single thistle standing tall. Its purple crown swayed gently in the breeze.

"You cannot feed me," said the stag. "No," replied the thistle, "but I can remind you that beauty grows even in the harshest ground."

The stag bowed his head and moved on, but the image of the thistle stayed with him.

That winter, when snow covered the meadows, it was the memory of that stubborn, bright flower that warmed his heart. A reminder that resilience can be its own kind of nourishment.

GOOD MORNING

DAY & DATE: ....

Today's Rune

WHAT GUIDANCE IS THIS RUNE GIVING ME TODAY?

_____
_____
_____
_____
_____

HOW IM FEELI ABOUT THIS D

- ☐ Happy
- ☐ Joyful
- ☐ Positive
- ☐ Energise
- ☐ Sad
- ☐ Angry
- ☐ Anguish
- ☐ Unhappy

TODAY GRATEFUL FOR:

1. _____
2. _____
3. _____

MY FOCUS FOR TODAY:

_____
_____
_____

How can today's rune help me make the most of today

GOOD EVENING

WHAT FELT IN HARMONY TODAY?

_____
_____
_____

WHAT FELT OUT OF BALANCE TODAY?

_____
_____
_____

WAS MY ENER WELL SPEN TODAY?

- ☐ Unfocused
- ☐ Distracted
- ☐ Steady
- ☐ Motivated
- ☐ Fully Engag

HOW DID THE ENERGY OR MEANING OF TODAY'S RUNE REVEAL ITSE

_____
_____

What small action I can take tomorrow to support m wellbeing...

GOOD MORNING

DAY & DATE: ....

Today's Rune

WHAT GUIDANCE IS THIS RUNE GIVING ME TODAY?

_____
_____
_____
_____

HOW IM FEELING ABOUT THIS DRAW?
- ☐ Happy
- ☐ Joyful
- ☐ Positive
- ☐ Energised
- ☐ Sad
- ☐ Angry
- ☐ Anguish
- ☐ Unhappy

TODAY GRATEFUL FOR:

_____
_____
_____

MY FOCUS FOR TODAY:

_____
_____
_____

How can today's rune help me make the most of today?

GOOD EVENING

WHAT FELT IN HARMONY TODAY?

_____
_____
_____

WHAT FELT OUT OF BALANCE TODAY?

_____
_____

WAS MY ENERGY WELL SPENT TODAY?
- ☐ Unfocused
- ☐ Distracted
- ☐ Steady
- ☐ Motivated
- ☐ Fully Engaged

HOW DID THE ENERGY OR MEANING OF TODAY'S RUNE REVEAL ITSELF?

_____
_____

What small action I can take tomorrow to support my wellbeing...

GOOD MORNING   DAY & DATE: _____

Today's Rune

WHAT GUIDANCE IS THIS RUNE GIVING ME TODAY?
_____
_____
_____
_____
_____

HOW IM FEELI ABOUT THIS DR
- ☐ Happy
- ☐ Joyful
- ☐ Positive
- ☐ Energised
- ☐ Sad
- ☐ Angry
- ☐ Anguish
- ☐ Unhappy

TODAY GRATEFUL FOR:
1. _____
2. _____
3. _____

MY FOCUS FOR TODAY:
_____
_____
_____

How can today's rune help me make the most of today

GOOD EVENING

WHAT FELT IN HARMONY TODAY?
_____
_____
_____

WHAT FELT OUT OF BALANCE TODAY?
_____
_____
_____

WAS MY ENER WELL SPEN TODAY?
- ☐ Unfocused
- ☐ Distracted
- ☐ Steady
- ☐ Motivated
- ☐ Fully Engag

HOW DID THE ENERGY OR MEANING OF TODAY'S RUNE REVEAL ITSE
_____
_____

What small action I can take tomorrow to support m wellbeing…

GOOD MORNING   DAY & DATE: ....

Today's Rune

WHAT GUIDANCE IS THIS RUNE GIVING ME TODAY?

_____
_____
_____
_____
_____

HOW IM FEELING ABOUT THIS DRAW?
☐ Happy
☐ Joyful
☐ Positive
☐ Energised
☐ Sad
☐ Angry
☐ Anguish
☐ Unhappy

TODAY GRATEFUL FOR:
_____
_____
_____

MY FOCUS FOR TODAY:
_____
_____
_____

How can today's rune help me make the most of today?

GOOD EVENING

WHAT FELT IN HARMONY TODAY?
_____
_____
_____

WAS MY ENERGY WELL SPENT TODAY?
☐ Unfocused
☐ Distracted
☐ Steady
☐ Motivated
☐ Fully Engaged

WHAT FELT OUT OF BALANCE TODAY?
_____
_____
_____

HOW DID THE ENERGY OR MEANING OF TODAY'S RUNE REVEAL ITSELF?
_____
_____

What small action I can take tomorrow to support my wellbeing…

GOOD MORNING   DAY & DATE: ....

Today's Rune

WHAT GUIDANCE IS THIS RUNE GIVING ME TODAY?

_____
_____
_____
_____
_____
_____

HOW IM FEELI[NG] ABOUT THIS D[AY]
- ☐ Happy
- ☐ Joyful
- ☐ Positive
- ☐ Energise[d]
- ☐ Sad
- ☐ Angry
- ☐ Anguish
- ☐ Unhappy

TODAY GRATEFUL FOR:

1. _____
2. _____
3. _____

MY FOCUS FOR TODAY:

_____
_____
_____

How can today's rune help me make the most of today[?]

GOOD EVENING

WHAT FELT IN HARMONY TODAY?

_____
_____
_____

WHAT FELT OUT OF BALANCE TODAY?

_____
_____
_____

WAS MY ENER[GY] WELL SPEN[T] TODAY?
- ☐ Unfocused
- ☐ Distracted
- ☐ Steady
- ☐ Motivated
- ☐ Fully Engag[ed]

HOW DID THE ENERGY OR MEANING OF TODAY'S RUNE REVEAL ITSE[LF?]

_____
_____

What small action I can take tomorrow to support m[y] wellbeing...

GOOD MORNING   DAY & DATE: ....

Today's Rune

WHAT GUIDANCE IS THIS RUNE GIVING ME TODAY?
_____
_____
_____
_____

HOW IM FEELING ABOUT THIS DRAW?
☐ Happy
☐ Joyful
☐ Positive
☐ Energised
☐ Sad
☐ Angry
☐ Anguish
☐ Unhappy

TODAY GRATEFUL FOR:
_____
_____
_____

MY FOCUS FOR TODAY:
_____
_____
_____

How can today's rune help me make the most of today?

GOOD EVENING

WHAT FELT IN HARMONY TODAY?
_____
_____
_____

WHAT FELT OUT OF BALANCE TODAY?
_____
_____

WAS MY ENERGY WELL SPENT TODAY?
☐ Unfocused
☐ Distracted
☐ Steady
☐ Motivated
☐ Fully Engaged

HOW DID THE ENERGY OR MEANING OF TODAY'S RUNE REVEAL ITSELF?
_____
_____

What small action I can take tomorrow to support my wellbeing…

GOOD MORNING

DAY & DATE: ....

Today's Rune

WHAT GUIDANCE IS THIS RUNE GIVING ME TODAY?

_____
_____
_____
_____
_____
_____

HOW IM FEELING ABOUT THIS D[AY]

- ☐ Happy
- ☐ Joyful
- ☐ Positive
- ☐ Energised
- ☐ Sad
- ☐ Angry
- ☐ Anguish
- ☐ Unhappy

TODAY GRATEFUL FOR:

1. _____
2. _____
3. _____

MY FOCUS FOR TODAY:

_____
_____
_____

How can today's rune help me make the most of today

GOOD EVENING

WHAT FELT IN HARMONY TODAY?

_____
_____
_____

WHAT FELT OUT OF BALANCE TODAY?

_____
_____
_____

WAS MY ENER[GY] WELL SPEN[T] TODAY?

- ☐ Unfocused
- ☐ Distracted
- ☐ Steady
- ☐ Motivated
- ☐ Fully Engag[ed]

HOW DID THE ENERGY OR MEANING OF TODAY'S RUNE REVEAL ITSE[LF]

_____
_____

What small action I can take tomorrow to support m[y] wellbeing…

"The present moment is the only time over which we have dominion."

Thích Nhất Hạnh

GOOD MORNING

DAY & DATE: ....

Today's Rune

WHAT GUIDANCE IS THIS RUNE GIVING ME TODAY?

_____
_____
_____
_____
_____
_____

HOW IM FEELI ABOUT THIS DF

☐ Happy
☐ Joyful
☐ Positive
☐ Energised
☐ Sad
☐ Angry
☐ Anguish
☐ Unhappy

TODAY GRATEFUL FOR:

1. _____
2. _____
3. _____

MY FOCUS FOR TODAY:

_____
_____
_____

How can today's rune help me make the most of today

GOOD EVENING

WHAT FELT IN HARMONY TODAY?

_____
_____
_____

WHAT FELT OUT OF BALANCE TODAY?

_____
_____
_____

WAS MY ENER WELL SPEN TODAY?

☐ Unfocused
☐ Distracted
☐ Steady
☐ Motivated
☐ Fully Engag

HOW DID THE ENERGY OR MEANING OF TODAY'S RUNE REVEAL ITSE

_____
_____

What small action I can take tomorrow to support m wellbeing…

GOOD MORNING

DAY & DATE: ....

Today's Rune

WHAT GUIDANCE IS THIS RUNE GIVING ME TODAY?

_____

_____

_____

_____

HOW IM FEELING ABOUT THIS DRAW?

☐ Happy
☐ Joyful
☐ Positive
☐ Energised
☐ Sad
☐ Angry
☐ Anguish
☐ Unhappy

TODAY GRATEFUL FOR:

_____

_____

_____

MY FOCUS FOR TODAY:

_____

_____

_____

How can today's rune help me make the most of today?

GOOD EVENING

WHAT FELT IN HARMONY TODAY?

_____

_____

_____

WHAT FELT OUT OF BALANCE TODAY?

_____

_____

_____

WAS MY ENERGY WELL SPENT TODAY?

☐ Unfocused
☐ Distracted
☐ Steady
☐ Motivated
☐ Fully Engaged

HOW DID THE ENERGY OR MEANING OF TODAY'S RUNE REVEAL ITSELF?

_____

_____

What small action I can take tomorrow to support my wellbeing...

GOOD MORNING

DAY & DATE: ....

Today's Rune

WHAT GUIDANCE IS THIS RUNE GIVING ME TODAY?

_____
_____
_____
_____
_____

HOW IM FEELI ABOUT THIS D

- ☐ Happy
- ☐ Joyful
- ☐ Positive
- ☐ Energise
- ☐ Sad
- ☐ Angry
- ☐ Anguish
- ☐ Unhappy

TODAY GRATEFUL FOR:

1. _____
2. _____
3. _____

MY FOCUS FOR TODAY:

_____
_____
_____

How can today's rune help me make the most of today

GOOD EVENING

WHAT FELT IN HARMONY TODAY?

_____
_____
_____

WHAT FELT OUT OF BALANCE TODAY?

_____
_____
_____

WAS MY ENEF WELL SPEN TODAY?

- ☐ Unfocused
- ☐ Distracted
- ☐ Steady
- ☐ Motivated
- ☐ Fully Engag

HOW DID THE ENERGY OR MEANING OF TODAY'S RUNE REVEAL ITSE

_____
_____

What small action I can take tomorrow to support m wellbeing...

OD MORNING   DAY & DATE: ....

WHAT GUIDANCE IS THIS RUNE GIVING ME TODAY?

_____

_____

_____

_____

Today's Rune

HOW IM FEELING ABOUT THIS DRAW?
☐ Happy
☐ Joyful
☐ Positive
☐ Energised
☐ Sad
☐ Angry
☐ Anguish
☐ Unhappy

DAY GRATEFUL FOR:

_____

_____

_____

MY FOCUS FOR TODAY:

_____

_____

_____

How can today's rune help me make the most of today?

OD EVENING

AT FELT IN HARMONY TODAY?

_____

_____

_____

WAS MY ENERGY WELL SPENT TODAY?
☐ Unfocused
☐ Distracted
☐ Steady
☐ Motivated
☐ Fully Engaged

AT FELT OUT OF BALANCE TODAY?

_____

_____

_____

W DID THE ENERGY OR MEANING OF TODAY'S RUNE REVEAL ITSELF?

_____

_____

What small action I can take tomorrow to support my ellbeing…

GOOD MORNING

DAY & DATE: _____

Today's Rune

WHAT GUIDANCE IS THIS RUNE GIVING ME TODAY?

_____
_____
_____
_____
_____

HOW IM FEELI[NG] ABOUT THIS D[AY]

- ☐ Happy
- ☐ Joyful
- ☐ Positive
- ☐ Energise[d]
- ☐ Sad
- ☐ Angry
- ☐ Anguish
- ☐ Unhappy

TODAY GRATEFUL FOR:

1. _____
2. _____
3. _____

MY FOCUS FOR TODAY:

_____
_____
_____

How can today's rune help me make the most of today

GOOD EVENING

WHAT FELT IN HARMONY TODAY?

_____
_____
_____

WHAT FELT OUT OF BALANCE TODAY?

_____
_____
_____

WAS MY ENER[GY] WELL SPEN[T] TODAY?

- ☐ Unfocused
- ☐ Distracted
- ☐ Steady
- ☐ Motivated
- ☐ Fully Engag[ed]

HOW DID THE ENERGY OR MEANING OF TODAY'S RUNE REVEAL ITSE[LF]

_____
_____

What small action I can take tomorrow to support m[y] wellbeing…

GOOD MORNING   DAY & DATE: ....

Today's Rune

WHAT GUIDANCE IS THIS RUNE GIVING ME TODAY?

_____

_____

_____

_____

HOW IM FEELING ABOUT THIS DRAW?
- ☐ Happy
- ☐ Joyful
- ☐ Positive
- ☐ Energised
- ☐ Sad
- ☐ Angry
- ☐ Anguish
- ☐ Unhappy

TODAY GRATEFUL FOR:

_____

_____

MY FOCUS FOR TODAY:

_____

_____

> How can today's rune help me make the most of today?

GOOD EVENING

WHAT FELT IN HARMONY TODAY?

_____

_____

_____

WHAT FELT OUT OF BALANCE TODAY?

_____

_____

_____

WAS MY ENERGY WELL SPENT TODAY?
- ☐ Unfocused
- ☐ Distracted
- ☐ Steady
- ☐ Motivated
- ☐ Fully Engaged

HOW DID THE ENERGY OR MEANING OF TODAY'S RUNE REVEAL ITSELF?

_____

_____

What small action I can take tomorrow to support my wellbeing...

GOOD MORNING

DAY & DATE: _____

Today's Rune

WHAT GUIDANCE IS THIS RUNE GIVING ME TODAY?

_____
_____
_____
_____
_____

HOW IM FEELI ABOUT THIS DF
- ☐ Happy
- ☐ Joyful
- ☐ Positive
- ☐ Energised
- ☐ Sad
- ☐ Angry
- ☐ Anguish
- ☐ Unhappy

TODAY GRATEFUL FOR:

1. _____
2. _____
3. _____

MY FOCUS FOR TODAY:

_____
_____
_____

How can today's rune help me make the most of today

GOOD EVENING

WHAT FELT IN HARMONY TODAY?

_____
_____
_____

WHAT FELT OUT OF BALANCE TODAY?

_____
_____
_____

WAS MY ENER WELL SPEN TODAY?
- ☐ Unfocused
- ☐ Distracted
- ☐ Steady
- ☐ Motivated
- ☐ Fully Engag

HOW DID THE ENERGY OR MEANING OF TODAY'S RUNE REVEAL ITSE

_____
_____

What small action I can take tomorrow to support m wellbeing...

Story time

The Blackbird's Pause

It was just after dawn when a blackbird began to sing from the edge of the forest. Its voice was clear, rich, and utterly unhurried, as though it had all the time in the world.

Along the path came a weary traveller, their mind heavy with the list of tasks ahead, each step quick and determined to reach some unseen finish line.

Then, they heard the blackbird.

The traveller stopped, listening. The forest seemed to hold its breath, the light soft and gold through the leaves. For a long moment, there was no road no pack, no deadlines — only the song.

When the blackbird fell silent, the traveller walked on. But their step was lighter now, as though they carried less weight.

Sometimes, the traveller realised, stopping is the fastest way forward.

GOOD MORNING

DAY & DATE: _____

Today's Rune

WHAT GUIDANCE IS THIS RUNE GIVING ME TODAY?

_____
_____
_____
_____
_____

HOW IM FEELI ABOUT THIS D

☐ Happy
☐ Joyful
☐ Positive
☐ Energise
☐ Sad
☐ Angry
☐ Anguish
☐ Unhappy

TODAY GRATEFUL FOR:

1. _____
2. _____
3. _____

MY FOCUS FOR TODAY:

_____
_____
_____

How can today's rune help me make the most of today

GOOD EVENING

WHAT FELT IN HARMONY TODAY?

_____
_____
_____

WHAT FELT OUT OF BALANCE TODAY?

_____
_____
_____

WAS MY ENEF WELL SPEN TODAY?

☐ Unfocused
☐ Distracted
☐ Steady
☐ Motivated
☐ Fully Engag

HOW DID THE ENERGY OR MEANING OF TODAY'S RUNE REVEAL ITSE

_____
_____

What small action I can take tomorrow to support m wellbeing…

OD MORNING

DAY & DATE: ....

WHAT GUIDANCE IS THIS RUNE GIVING ME TODAY?

_____
_____
_____
_____
_____

Today's Rune

HOW IM FEELING ABOUT THIS DRAW?
- ☐ Happy
- ☐ Joyful
- ☐ Positive
- ☐ Energised
- ☐ Sad
- ☐ Angry
- ☐ Anguish
- ☐ Unhappy

DAY GRATEFUL FOR:

_____
_____
_____

MY FOCUS FOR TODAY:

_____
_____
_____

How can today's rune help me make the most of today?

OD EVENING

AT FELT IN HARMONY TODAY?

_____
_____
_____

WAS MY ENERGY WELL SPENT TODAY?
- ☐ Unfocused
- ☐ Distracted
- ☐ Steady
- ☐ Motivated
- ☐ Fully Engaged

AT FELT OUT OF BALANCE TODAY?

_____
_____

W DID THE ENERGY OR MEANING OF TODAY'S RUNE REVEAL ITSELF?

_____
_____

What small action I can take tomorrow to support my ellbeing…

GOOD MORNING

DAY & DATE: _____

Today's Rune

WHAT GUIDANCE IS THIS RUNE GIVING ME TODAY?
_____
_____
_____
_____
_____
_____

HOW IM FEELI ABOUT THIS D
- ☐ Happy
- ☐ Joyful
- ☐ Positive
- ☐ Energise
- ☐ Sad
- ☐ Angry
- ☐ Anguish
- ☐ Unhappy

TODAY GRATEFUL FOR:

1. _____
2. _____
3. _____

MY FOCUS FOR TODAY:

_____
_____
_____

How can today's rune help me make the most of today

GOOD EVENING

WHAT FELT IN HARMONY TODAY?
_____
_____
_____

WHAT FELT OUT OF BALANCE TODAY?
_____
_____
_____

WAS MY ENER WELL SPEN TODAY?
- ☐ Unfocused
- ☐ Distracted
- ☐ Steady
- ☐ Motivated
- ☐ Fully Engag

HOW DID THE ENERGY OR MEANING OF TODAY'S RUNE REVEAL ITSE
_____
_____

What small action I can take tomorrow to support m wellbeing...

GOOD MORNING

DAY & DATE: ....

WHAT GUIDANCE IS THIS RUNE GIVING ME TODAY?

_____
_____
_____
_____

Today's Rune

HOW IM FEELING ABOUT THIS DRAW?
- ☐ Happy
- ☐ Joyful
- ☐ Positive
- ☐ Energised
- ☐ Sad
- ☐ Angry
- ☐ Anguish
- ☐ Unhappy

TODAY GRATEFUL FOR:
_____
_____
_____

MY FOCUS FOR TODAY:
_____
_____
_____

How can today's rune help me make the most of today?

GOOD EVENING

WHAT FELT IN HARMONY TODAY?
_____
_____
_____

WAS MY ENERGY WELL SPENT TODAY?
- ☐ Unfocused
- ☐ Distracted
- ☐ Steady
- ☐ Motivated
- ☐ Fully Engaged

WHAT FELT OUT OF BALANCE TODAY?
_____
_____
_____

HOW DID THE ENERGY OR MEANING OF TODAY'S RUNE REVEAL ITSELF?
_____
_____

What small action I can take tomorrow to support my wellbeing…

GOOD MORNING

DAY & DATE: _____

Today's Rune

WHAT GUIDANCE IS THIS RUNE GIVING ME TODAY?
_____
_____
_____
_____
_____

HOW IM FEELI ABOUT THIS DA
- ☐ Happy
- ☐ Joyful
- ☐ Positive
- ☐ Energised
- ☐ Sad
- ☐ Angry
- ☐ Anguish
- ☐ Unhappy

TODAY GRATEFUL FOR:

1. _____
2. _____
3. _____

MY FOCUS FOR TODAY:
_____
_____
_____

How can today's rune help me make the most of today

GOOD EVENING

WHAT FELT IN HARMONY TODAY?
_____
_____
_____

WHAT FELT OUT OF BALANCE TODAY?
_____
_____
_____

WAS MY ENER WELL SPEN TODAY?
- ☐ Unfocused
- ☐ Distracted
- ☐ Steady
- ☐ Motivated
- ☐ Fully Engag

HOW DID THE ENERGY OR MEANING OF TODAY'S RUNE REVEAL ITSE
_____
_____
_____

What small action I can take tomorrow to support m wellbeing...

GOOD MORNING   DAY & DATE: _____

WHAT GUIDANCE IS THIS RUNE GIVING ME TODAY?

_____
_____
_____
_____

Today's Rune

HOW IM FEELING ABOUT THIS DRAW?
☐ Happy
☐ Joyful
☐ Positive
☐ Energised
☐ Sad
☐ Angry
☐ Anguish
☐ Unhappy

TODAY GRATEFUL FOR:
_____
_____
_____

MY FOCUS FOR TODAY:
_____
_____
_____

How can today's rune help me make the most of today?

GOOD EVENING

WHAT FELT IN HARMONY TODAY?
_____
_____
_____

WHAT FELT OUT OF BALANCE TODAY?
_____
_____
_____

WAS MY ENERGY WELL SPENT TODAY?
☐ Unfocused
☐ Distracted
☐ Steady
☐ Motivated
☐ Fully Engaged

HOW DID THE ENERGY OR MEANING OF TODAY'S RUNE REVEAL ITSELF?
_____
_____

What small action I can take tomorrow to support my wellbeing...

GOOD MORNING

DAY & DATE: ....

Today's Rune

WHAT GUIDANCE IS THIS RUNE GIVING ME TODAY?

_____
_____
_____
_____
_____

HOW IM FEELING ABOUT THIS DAY

☐ Happy
☐ Joyful
☐ Positive
☐ Energised
☐ Sad
☐ Angry
☐ Anguish
☐ Unhappy

TODAY GRATEFUL FOR:

1. _____
2. _____
3. _____

MY FOCUS FOR TODAY:

_____
_____
_____

How can today's rune help me make the most of today

GOOD EVENING

WHAT FELT IN HARMONY TODAY?

_____
_____
_____

WHAT FELT OUT OF BALANCE TODAY?

_____
_____
_____

WAS MY ENERGY WELL SPENT TODAY?

☐ Unfocused
☐ Distracted
☐ Steady
☐ Motivated
☐ Fully Engaged

HOW DID THE ENERGY OR MEANING OF TODAY'S RUNE REVEAL ITSELF

_____
_____

What small action I can take tomorrow to support my wellbeing…

RUNES ARE NOT SIMPLY READ — THEY ARE FELT, LIVED, AND CARRIED WITH YOU.

GOOD MORNING

DAY & DATE: _____

Today's Rune

WHAT GUIDANCE IS THIS RUNE GIVING ME TODAY?
_____
_____
_____
_____
_____

HOW IM FEELI[NG] ABOUT THIS D[AY]
- ☐ Happy
- ☐ Joyful
- ☐ Positive
- ☐ Energise[d]
- ☐ Sad
- ☐ Angry
- ☐ Anguish
- ☐ Unhappy

TODAY GRATEFUL FOR:
1. _____
2. _____
3. _____

MY FOCUS FOR TODAY:
_____
_____
_____

How can today's rune help me make the most of today

GOOD EVENING

WHAT FELT IN HARMONY TODAY?
_____
_____
_____

WHAT FELT OUT OF BALANCE TODAY?
_____
_____
_____

WAS MY ENER[GY] WELL SPEN[T] TODAY?
- ☐ Unfocused
- ☐ Distracted
- ☐ Steady
- ☐ Motivated
- ☐ Fully Engag[ed]

HOW DID THE ENERGY OR MEANING OF TODAY'S RUNE REVEAL ITSE[LF]
_____
_____

What small action I can take tomorrow to support m[y] wellbeing…

GOOD MORNING

DAY & DATE: ....

Today's Rune

WHAT GUIDANCE IS THIS RUNE GIVING ME TODAY?

_____

_____

_____

_____

HOW IM FEELING ABOUT THIS DRAW?
- ☐ Happy
- ☐ Joyful
- ☐ Positive
- ☐ Energised
- ☐ Sad
- ☐ Angry
- ☐ Anguish
- ☐ Unhappy

TODAY GRATEFUL FOR:

MY FOCUS FOR TODAY:

How can today's rune help me make the most of today?

GOOD EVENING

WHAT FELT IN HARMONY TODAY?

_____

_____

_____

WHAT FELT OUT OF BALANCE TODAY?

_____

_____

_____

WAS MY ENERGY WELL SPENT TODAY?
- ☐ Unfocused
- ☐ Distracted
- ☐ Steady
- ☐ Motivated
- ☐ Fully Engaged

HOW DID THE ENERGY OR MEANING OF TODAY'S RUNE REVEAL ITSELF?

What small action I can take tomorrow to support my wellbeing...

GOOD MORNING

DAY & DATE: _____

Today's Rune

WHAT GUIDANCE IS THIS RUNE GIVING ME TODAY?
_____
_____
_____
_____
_____

HOW IM FEELI ABOUT THIS D
- ☐ Happy
- ☐ Joyful
- ☐ Positive
- ☐ Energised
- ☐ Sad
- ☐ Angry
- ☐ Anguish
- ☐ Unhappy

TODAY GRATEFUL FOR:
1. _____
2. _____
3. _____

MY FOCUS FOR TODAY:
_____
_____
_____

How can today's rune help me make the most of today

GOOD EVENING

WHAT FELT IN HARMONY TODAY?
_____
_____
_____

WHAT FELT OUT OF BALANCE TODAY?
_____
_____
_____

WAS MY ENER WELL SPEN TODAY?
- ☐ Unfocused
- ☐ Distracted
- ☐ Steady
- ☐ Motivated
- ☐ Fully Engag

HOW DID THE ENERGY OR MEANING OF TODAY'S RUNE REVEAL ITSE
_____
_____

What small action I can take tomorrow to support m wellbeing...

OD MORNING

DAY & DATE: ....

WHAT GUIDANCE IS THIS RUNE GIVING ME TODAY?

_____

_____

_____

_____

Today's Rune

HOW IM FEELING ABOUT THIS DRAW?
☐ Happy
☐ Joyful
☐ Positive
☐ Energised
☐ Sad
☐ Angry
☐ Anguish
☐ Unhappy

DAY GRATEFUL FOR:

_____

_____

_____

MY FOCUS FOR TODAY:

_____

_____

_____

How can today's rune help me make the most of today?

OD EVENING

AT FELT IN HARMONY TODAY?

_____

_____

_____

AT FELT OUT OF BALANCE TODAY?

_____

_____

_____

WAS MY ENERGY WELL SPENT TODAY?
☐ Unfocused
☐ Distracted
☐ Steady
☐ Motivated
☐ Fully Engaged

W DID THE ENERGY OR MEANING OF TODAY'S RUNE REVEAL ITSELF?

_____

_____

hat small action I can take tomorrow to support my ellbeing...

GOOD MORNING

DAY & DATE: _____

Today's Rune

WHAT GUIDANCE IS THIS RUNE GIVING ME TODAY?

_____
_____
_____
_____
_____

HOW IM FEELI[NG] ABOUT THIS D[AY]

- ☐ Happy
- ☐ Joyful
- ☐ Positive
- ☐ Energise[d]
- ☐ Sad
- ☐ Angry
- ☐ Anguish
- ☐ Unhappy

TODAY GRATEFUL FOR:

1. _____
2. _____
3. _____

MY FOCUS FOR TODAY:

_____
_____
_____

How can today's rune help me make the most of today[?]

GOOD EVENING

WHAT FELT IN HARMONY TODAY?

_____
_____
_____

WHAT FELT OUT OF BALANCE TODAY?

_____
_____
_____

WAS MY ENER[GY] WELL SPEN[T] TODAY?

- ☐ Unfocused
- ☐ Distracted
- ☐ Steady
- ☐ Motivated
- ☐ Fully Engag[ed]

HOW DID THE ENERGY OR MEANING OF TODAY'S RUNE REVEAL ITSE[LF?]

_____
_____

What small action I can take tomorrow to support m[y] wellbeing…

OD MORNING   DAY & DATE: _____

WHAT GUIDANCE IS THIS RUNE GIVING ME TODAY?

_____
_____
_____
_____

Today's Rune

HOW IM FEELING ABOUT THIS DRAW?
- ☐ Happy
- ☐ Joyful
- ☐ Positive
- ☐ Energised
- ☐ Sad
- ☐ Angry
- ☐ Anguish
- ☐ Unhappy

DAY GRATEFUL FOR:
_____
_____
_____

MY FOCUS FOR TODAY:
_____
_____
_____

How can today's rune help me make the most of today?

OD EVENING

WHAT FELT IN HARMONY TODAY?
_____
_____
_____

WAS MY ENERGY WELL SPENT TODAY?
- ☐ Unfocused
- ☐ Distracted
- ☐ Steady
- ☐ Motivated
- ☐ Fully Engaged

WHAT FELT OUT OF BALANCE TODAY?
_____
_____
_____

HOW DID THE ENERGY OR MEANING OF TODAY'S RUNE REVEAL ITSELF?
_____
_____

What small action I can take tomorrow to support my wellbeing…

GOOD MORNING

DAY & DATE: _____

Today's Rune

WHAT GUIDANCE IS THIS RUNE GIVING ME TODAY?
_____
_____
_____
_____
_____

HOW IM FEELING ABOUT THIS DAY
- ☐ Happy
- ☐ Joyful
- ☐ Positive
- ☐ Energised
- ☐ Sad
- ☐ Angry
- ☐ Anguish
- ☐ Unhappy

TODAY GRATEFUL FOR:

1. _____
2. _____
3. _____

MY FOCUS FOR TODAY:
_____
_____
_____

How can today's rune help me make the most of today

GOOD EVENING

WHAT FELT IN HARMONY TODAY?
_____
_____
_____

WHAT FELT OUT OF BALANCE TODAY?
_____
_____
_____
_____

WAS MY ENERGY WELL SPENT TODAY?
- ☐ Unfocused
- ☐ Distracted
- ☐ Steady
- ☐ Motivated
- ☐ Fully Engaged

HOW DID THE ENERGY OR MEANING OF TODAY'S RUNE REVEAL ITSELF
_____
_____

What small action I can take tomorrow to support my wellbeing...

>

"Even the smallest pause can change the course of your day."

Anon

GOOD MORNING

DAY & DATE: _____

Today's Rune

WHAT GUIDANCE IS THIS RUNE GIVING ME TODAY?
_____
_____
_____
_____
_____

HOW IM FEELI ABOUT THIS DF
- ☐ Happy
- ☐ Joyful
- ☐ Positive
- ☐ Energised
- ☐ Sad
- ☐ Angry
- ☐ Anguish
- ☐ Unhappy

TODAY GRATEFUL FOR:
1. _____
2. _____
3. _____

MY FOCUS FOR TODAY:
_____
_____
_____

How can today's rune help me make the most of today

GOOD EVENING

WHAT FELT IN HARMONY TODAY?
_____
_____
_____

WHAT FELT OUT OF BALANCE TODAY?
_____
_____
_____

WAS MY ENER WELL SPEN TODAY?
- ☐ Unfocused
- ☐ Distracted
- ☐ Steady
- ☐ Motivated
- ☐ Fully Engag

HOW DID THE ENERGY OR MEANING OF TODAY'S RUNE REVEAL ITSE
_____
_____

What small action I can take tomorrow to support m wellbeing…

OD MORNING   DAY & DATE: ....

WHAT GUIDANCE IS THIS RUNE GIVING ME TODAY?

_____

_____

_____

_____

Today's Rune

HOW IM FEELING ABOUT THIS DRAW?
- ☐ Happy
- ☐ Joyful
- ☐ Positive
- ☐ Energised
- ☐ Sad
- ☐ Angry
- ☐ Anguish
- ☐ Unhappy

DAY GRATEFUL FOR:
_____
_____
_____

MY FOCUS FOR TODAY:
_____
_____
_____

> How can today's rune help me make the most of today?

OD EVENING

AT FELT IN HARMONY TODAY?
_____
_____
_____

WAS MY ENERGY WELL SPENT TODAY?
- ☐ Unfocused
- ☐ Distracted
- ☐ Steady
- ☐ Motivated
- ☐ Fully Engaged

AT FELT OUT OF BALANCE TODAY?
_____
_____
_____

W DID THE ENERGY OR MEANING OF TODAY'S RUNE REVEAL ITSELF?
_____
_____

> hat small action I can take tomorrow to support my ellbeing…

GOOD MORNING

DAY & DATE: _____

Today's Rune

WHAT GUIDANCE IS THIS RUNE GIVING ME TODAY?

_____
_____
_____
_____
_____

HOW IM FEELING ABOUT THIS DAY

- ☐ Happy
- ☐ Joyful
- ☐ Positive
- ☐ Energised
- ☐ Sad
- ☐ Angry
- ☐ Anguish
- ☐ Unhappy

TODAY GRATEFUL FOR:

1. _____
2. _____
3. _____

MY FOCUS FOR TODAY:

_____
_____
_____

How can today's rune help me make the most of today

GOOD EVENING

WHAT FELT IN HARMONY TODAY?

_____
_____
_____

WHAT FELT OUT OF BALANCE TODAY?

_____
_____
_____

WAS MY ENERGY WELL SPENT TODAY?

- ☐ Unfocused
- ☐ Distracted
- ☐ Steady
- ☐ Motivated
- ☐ Fully Engaged

HOW DID THE ENERGY OR MEANING OF TODAY'S RUNE REVEAL ITSELF

_____
_____

What small action I can take tomorrow to support my wellbeing…

GOOD MORNING

DAY & DATE: ....

Today's Rune

WHAT GUIDANCE IS THIS RUNE GIVING ME TODAY?

_____
_____
_____
_____
_____

HOW IM FEELING ABOUT THIS DRAW?

☐ Happy
☐ Joyful
☐ Positive
☐ Energised
☐ Sad
☐ Angry
☐ Anguish
☐ Unhappy

TODAY GRATEFUL FOR:

_____
_____
_____

MY FOCUS FOR TODAY:

_____
_____
_____

How can today's rune help me make the most of today?

GOOD EVENING

WHAT FELT IN HARMONY TODAY?

_____
_____
_____

WAS MY ENERGY WELL SPENT TODAY?

☐ Unfocused
☐ Distracted
☐ Steady
☐ Motivated
☐ Fully Engaged

WHAT FELT OUT OF BALANCE TODAY?

_____
_____
_____

HOW DID THE ENERGY OR MEANING OF TODAY'S RUNE REVEAL ITSELF?

_____
_____

What small action I can take tomorrow to support my wellbeing…

GOOD MORNING

DAY & DATE: _____

Today's Rune

WHAT GUIDANCE IS THIS RUNE GIVING ME TODAY?
_____
_____
_____
_____
_____

HOW IM FEELI[NG] ABOUT THIS D[AY]
- ☐ Happy
- ☐ Joyful
- ☐ Positive
- ☐ Energise[d]
- ☐ Sad
- ☐ Angry
- ☐ Anguish
- ☐ Unhappy

TODAY GRATEFUL FOR:

1. _____
2. _____
3. _____

MY FOCUS FOR TODAY:

_____
_____
_____

How can today's rune help me make the most of today[?]

GOOD EVENING

WHAT FELT IN HARMONY TODAY?
_____
_____
_____

WHAT FELT OUT OF BALANCE TODAY?
_____
_____
_____

WAS MY ENE[RGY] WELL SPEN[T] TODAY?
- ☐ Unfocused
- ☐ Distracted
- ☐ Steady
- ☐ Motivated
- ☐ Fully Engag[ed]

HOW DID THE ENERGY OR MEANING OF TODAY'S RUNE REVEAL ITSE[LF]
_____
_____

What small action I can take tomorrow to support m[y] wellbeing...

GOOD MORNING

DAY & DATE: _____

WHAT GUIDANCE IS THIS RUNE GIVING ME TODAY?

_____
_____
_____
_____

HOW IM FEELING ABOUT THIS DRAW?
- ☐ Happy
- ☐ Joyful
- ☐ Positive
- ☐ Energised
- ☐ Sad
- ☐ Angry
- ☐ Anguish
- ☐ Unhappy

Today's Rune

TODAY GRATEFUL FOR:

_____
_____
_____

MY FOCUS FOR TODAY:

_____
_____
_____

How can today's rune help me make the most of today?

GOOD EVENING

WHAT FELT IN HARMONY TODAY?

_____
_____
_____

WHAT FELT OUT OF BALANCE TODAY?

_____
_____
_____

WAS MY ENERGY WELL SPENT TODAY?
- ☐ Unfocused
- ☐ Distracted
- ☐ Steady
- ☐ Motivated
- ☐ Fully Engaged

HOW DID THE ENERGY OR MEANING OF TODAY'S RUNE REVEAL ITSELF?

_____
_____

What small action I can take tomorrow to support my wellbeing…

GOOD MORNING

DAY & DATE: _____

Today's Rune

WHAT GUIDANCE IS THIS RUNE GIVING ME TODAY?

_____
_____
_____
_____
_____

HOW IM FEELI ABOUT THIS DF
- ☐ Happy
- ☐ Joyful
- ☐ Positive
- ☐ Energised
- ☐ Sad
- ☐ Angry
- ☐ Anguish
- ☐ Unhappy

TODAY GRATEFUL FOR:

1. _____
2. _____
3. _____

MY FOCUS FOR TODAY:

_____
_____
_____

How can today's rune help me make the most of today

GOOD EVENING

WHAT FELT IN HARMONY TODAY?

_____
_____
_____

WHAT FELT OUT OF BALANCE TODAY?

_____
_____

WAS MY ENER WELL SPEN TODAY?
- ☐ Unfocused
- ☐ Distracted
- ☐ Steady
- ☐ Motivated
- ☐ Fully Engag

HOW DID THE ENERGY OR MEANING OF TODAY'S RUNE REVEAL ITSE

_____
_____

What small action I can take tomorrow to support m wellbeing…

*Breathe.
This moment will never come again.*

GOOD MORNING

DAY & DATE: ....

Today's Rune

WHAT GUIDANCE IS THIS RUNE GIVING ME TODAY?

_____
_____
_____
_____
_____

HOW IM FEELING ABOUT THIS D

- ☐ Happy
- ☐ Joyful
- ☐ Positive
- ☐ Energised
- ☐ Sad
- ☐ Angry
- ☐ Anguish
- ☐ Unhappy

TODAY GRATEFUL FOR:

1. _____
2. _____
3. _____

MY FOCUS FOR TODAY:

_____
_____
_____

How can today's rune help me make the most of today

GOOD EVENING

WHAT FELT IN HARMONY TODAY?

_____
_____
_____

WHAT FELT OUT OF BALANCE TODAY?

_____
_____
_____

WAS MY ENERGY WELL SPENT TODAY?

- ☐ Unfocused
- ☐ Distracted
- ☐ Steady
- ☐ Motivated
- ☐ Fully Engag

HOW DID THE ENERGY OR MEANING OF TODAY'S RUNE REVEAL ITSE

_____
_____

What small action I can take tomorrow to support m wellbeing...

OD MORNING   DAY & DATE: ....

Today's Rune

WHAT GUIDANCE IS THIS RUNE GIVING ME TODAY?
_____
_____
_____
_____

HOW IM FEELING ABOUT THIS DRAW?
☐ Happy
☐ Joyful
☐ Positive
☐ Energised
☐ Sad
☐ Angry
☐ Anguish
☐ Unhappy

DAY GRATEFUL FOR:
_____
_____
_____

MY FOCUS FOR TODAY:
_____
_____
_____

How can today's rune help me make the most of today?

OD EVENING

AT FELT IN HARMONY TODAY?
_____
_____
_____

WAS MY ENERGY WELL SPENT TODAY?
☐ Unfocused
☐ Distracted
☐ Steady
☐ Motivated
☐ Fully Engaged

AT FELT OUT OF BALANCE TODAY?
_____
_____

W DID THE ENERGY OR MEANING OF TODAY'S RUNE REVEAL ITSELF?
_____
_____

hat small action I can take tomorrow to support my ellbeing...

GOOD MORNING

DAY & DATE: ....

Today's Rune

WHAT GUIDANCE IS THIS RUNE GIVING ME TODAY?

_____
_____
_____
_____
_____

HOW IM FEELING ABOUT THIS D[AY]

- ☐ Happy
- ☐ Joyful
- ☐ Positive
- ☐ Energised
- ☐ Sad
- ☐ Angry
- ☐ Anguish
- ☐ Unhappy

TODAY GRATEFUL FOR:

1. _____
2. _____
3. _____

MY FOCUS FOR TODAY:

_____
_____
_____

How can today's rune help me make the most of today

GOOD EVENING

WHAT FELT IN HARMONY TODAY?

_____
_____
_____

WHAT FELT OUT OF BALANCE TODAY?

_____
_____
_____

WAS MY ENERGY WELL SPENT TODAY?

- ☐ Unfocused
- ☐ Distracted
- ☐ Steady
- ☐ Motivated
- ☐ Fully Engag[ed]

HOW DID THE ENERGY OR MEANING OF TODAY'S RUNE REVEAL ITSE[LF]

_____

What small action I can take tomorrow to support m[y] wellbeing...

GOOD MORNING

DAY & DATE: ....

WHAT GUIDANCE IS THIS RUNE GIVING ME TODAY?

_____

_____

_____

_____

Today's Rune

HOW IM FEELING ABOUT THIS DRAW?
- ☐ Happy
- ☐ Joyful
- ☐ Positive
- ☐ Energised
- ☐ Sad
- ☐ Angry
- ☐ Anguish
- ☐ Unhappy

TODAY GRATEFUL FOR:

_____

_____

MY FOCUS FOR TODAY:

_____

_____

How can today's rune help me make the most of today?

GOOD EVENING

WHAT FELT IN HARMONY TODAY?

_____

_____

WHAT FELT OUT OF BALANCE TODAY?

_____

_____

WAS MY ENERGY WELL SPENT TODAY?
- ☐ Unfocused
- ☐ Distracted
- ☐ Steady
- ☐ Motivated
- ☐ Fully Engaged

HOW DID THE ENERGY OR MEANING OF TODAY'S RUNE REVEAL ITSELF?

_____

_____

What small action I can take tomorrow to support my wellbeing...

GOOD MORNING

DAY & DATE: _____

Today's Rune

WHAT GUIDANCE IS THIS RUNE GIVING ME TODAY?
_____
_____
_____
_____

HOW IM FEELI ABOUT THIS DF
- ☐ Happy
- ☐ Joyful
- ☐ Positive
- ☐ Energised
- ☐ Sad
- ☐ Angry
- ☐ Anguish
- ☐ Unhappy

TODAY GRATEFUL FOR:
1. _____
2. _____
3. _____

MY FOCUS FOR TODAY:
_____
_____
_____

How can today's rune help me make the most of today

GOOD EVENING

WHAT FELT IN HARMONY TODAY?
_____
_____
_____

WHAT FELT OUT OF BALANCE TODAY?
_____
_____
_____

WAS MY ENER WELL SPEN TODAY?
- ☐ Unfocused
- ☐ Distracted
- ☐ Steady
- ☐ Motivated
- ☐ Fully Engag

HOW DID THE ENERGY OR MEANING OF TODAY'S RUNE REVEAL ITSE
_____
_____

What small action I can take tomorrow to support m wellbeing…

GOOD MORNING

DAY & DATE: _____

Today's Rune

WHAT GUIDANCE IS THIS RUNE GIVING ME TODAY?

_____
_____
_____
_____

HOW IM FEELING ABOUT THIS DRAW?

☐ Happy
☐ Joyful
☐ Positive
☐ Energised
☐ Sad
☐ Angry
☐ Anguish
☐ Unhappy

TODAY GRATEFUL FOR:

_____
_____

MY FOCUS FOR TODAY:

_____
_____

How can today's rune help me make the most of today?

GOOD EVENING

WHAT FELT IN HARMONY TODAY?

_____
_____
_____

WHAT FELT OUT OF BALANCE TODAY?

_____
_____

WAS MY ENERGY WELL SPENT TODAY?

☐ Unfocused
☐ Distracted
☐ Steady
☐ Motivated
☐ Fully Engaged

HOW DID THE ENERGY OR MEANING OF TODAY'S RUNE REVEAL ITSELF?

_____
_____

What small action I can take tomorrow to support my wellbeing…

GOOD MORNING

DAY & DATE: _____

Today's Rune

WHAT GUIDANCE IS THIS RUNE GIVING ME TODAY?
_____
_____
_____
_____
_____

HOW IM FEELI[NG] ABOUT THIS D[AY]
- ☐ Happy
- ☐ Joyful
- ☐ Positive
- ☐ Energised
- ☐ Sad
- ☐ Angry
- ☐ Anguish
- ☐ Unhappy

TODAY GRATEFUL FOR:
1. _____
2. _____
3. _____

MY FOCUS FOR TODAY:
_____
_____
_____

How can today's rune help me make the most of today

GOOD EVENING

WHAT FELT IN HARMONY TODAY?
_____
_____
_____

WHAT FELT OUT OF BALANCE TODAY?
_____
_____
_____

WAS MY ENER[GY] WELL SPEN[T] TODAY?
- ☐ Unfocused
- ☐ Distracted
- ☐ Steady
- ☐ Motivated
- ☐ Fully Engag[ed]

HOW DID THE ENERGY OR MEANING OF TODAY'S RUNE REVEAL ITSE[LF]
_____
_____

What small action I can take tomorrow to support m[y] wellbeing...

Story time

The Lantern and the Path

The night was moonless, and the road ahead was swallowed in darkness. A traveller stood at the edge of the path, holding a lantern. Its glow was small, barely enough to see a few steps ahead.

"What if the light goes out?" they thought. "What if I get lost?"

They hesitated. The darkness was vast and quiet, pressing in on all sides.

But the lantern burned steadily, and so the traveller took one step, then another. Each time their foot found solid ground, the lantern revealed a little more. The path curved, dipped, and rose. Never fully in view, but always just enough to keep going.

By dawn, the traveller realised something they would never forget:

You don't need to see the whole road. You just need enough light to take the next step.

GOOD MORNING

DAY & DATE: _____

Today's Rune

WHAT GUIDANCE IS THIS RUNE GIVING ME TODAY?

_____
_____
_____
_____
_____

HOW IM FEELING ABOUT THIS DAY

- ☐ Happy
- ☐ Joyful
- ☐ Positive
- ☐ Energised
- ☐ Sad
- ☐ Angry
- ☐ Anguish
- ☐ Unhappy

TODAY GRATEFUL FOR:

1. _____
2. _____
3. _____

MY FOCUS FOR TODAY:

_____
_____
_____

How can today's rune help me make the most of today

GOOD EVENING

WHAT FELT IN HARMONY TODAY?

_____
_____
_____

WHAT FELT OUT OF BALANCE TODAY?

_____
_____
_____

WAS MY ENERGY WELL SPENT TODAY?

- ☐ Unfocused
- ☐ Distracted
- ☐ Steady
- ☐ Motivated
- ☐ Fully Engaged

HOW DID THE ENERGY OR MEANING OF TODAY'S RUNE REVEAL ITSELF

_____
_____

What small action I can take tomorrow to support my wellbeing…

GOOD MORNING

DAY & DATE: _____

Today's Rune

WHAT GUIDANCE IS THIS RUNE GIVING ME TODAY?

_____
_____
_____
_____

HOW IM FEELING ABOUT THIS DRAW?
- ☐ Happy
- ☐ Joyful
- ☐ Positive
- ☐ Energised
- ☐ Sad
- ☐ Angry
- ☐ Anguish
- ☐ Unhappy

TODAY GRATEFUL FOR:

_____
_____

MY FOCUS FOR TODAY:

_____
_____

How can today's rune help me make the most of today?

_____

GOOD EVENING

WHAT FELT IN HARMONY TODAY?

_____
_____

WHAT FELT OUT OF BALANCE TODAY?

_____
_____

WAS MY ENERGY WELL SPENT TODAY?
- ☐ Unfocused
- ☐ Distracted
- ☐ Steady
- ☐ Motivated
- ☐ Fully Engaged

HOW DID THE ENERGY OR MEANING OF TODAY'S RUNE REVEAL ITSELF?

_____
_____

What small action I can take tomorrow to support my wellbeing…

GOOD MORNING

DAY & DATE: _____

Today's Rune

WHAT GUIDANCE IS THIS RUNE GIVING ME TODAY?
_____
_____
_____
_____
_____

HOW IM FEELI ABOUT THIS DF
- ☐ Happy
- ☐ Joyful
- ☐ Positive
- ☐ Energised
- ☐ Sad
- ☐ Angry
- ☐ Anguish
- ☐ Unhappy

TODAY GRATEFUL FOR:
1. _____
2. _____
3. _____

MY FOCUS FOR TODAY:
_____
_____
_____

How can today's rune help me make the most of today

GOOD EVENING

WHAT FELT IN HARMONY TODAY?
_____
_____
_____

WHAT FELT OUT OF BALANCE TODAY?
_____
_____

WAS MY ENER WELL SPEN TODAY?
- ☐ Unfocused
- ☐ Distracted
- ☐ Steady
- ☐ Motivated
- ☐ Fully Engag

HOW DID THE ENERGY OR MEANING OF TODAY'S RUNE REVEAL ITSE

What small action I can take tomorrow to support m wellbeing…

OD MORNING

DAY & DATE: ....

WHAT GUIDANCE IS THIS RUNE GIVING ME TODAY?

_____

_____

_____

_____

Today's Rune

HOW IM FEELING ABOUT THIS DRAW?
- ☐ Happy
- ☐ Joyful
- ☐ Positive
- ☐ Energised
- ☐ Sad
- ☐ Angry
- ☐ Anguish
- ☐ Unhappy

DAY GRATEFUL FOR:

_____

_____

_____

MY FOCUS FOR TODAY:

_____

_____

_____

How can today's rune help me make the most of today?

OD EVENING

AT FELT IN HARMONY TODAY?

_____

_____

_____

AT FELT OUT OF BALANCE TODAY?

_____

_____

_____

WAS MY ENERGY WELL SPENT TODAY?
- ☐ Unfocused
- ☐ Distracted
- ☐ Steady
- ☐ Motivated
- ☐ Fully Engaged

W DID THE ENERGY OR MEANING OF TODAY'S RUNE REVEAL ITSELF?

_____

_____

hat small action I can take tomorrow to support my ellbeing…

GOOD MORNING

DAY & DATE: ....

Today's Rune

WHAT GUIDANCE IS THIS RUNE GIVING ME TODAY?

_____
_____
_____
_____
_____

HOW IM FEELING ABOUT THIS DAY
- ☐ Happy
- ☐ Joyful
- ☐ Positive
- ☐ Energised
- ☐ Sad
- ☐ Angry
- ☐ Anguish
- ☐ Unhappy

TODAY GRATEFUL FOR:

1. _____
2. _____
3. _____

MY FOCUS FOR TODAY:

_____
_____
_____

How can today's rune help me make the most of today

GOOD EVENING

WHAT FELT IN HARMONY TODAY?

_____
_____
_____

WHAT FELT OUT OF BALANCE TODAY?

_____
_____
_____

WAS MY ENERGY WELL SPENT TODAY?
- ☐ Unfocused
- ☐ Distracted
- ☐ Steady
- ☐ Motivated
- ☐ Fully Engaged

HOW DID THE ENERGY OR MEANING OF TODAY'S RUNE REVEAL ITSELF

_____
_____

What small action I can take tomorrow to support my wellbeing...

OD MORNING   DAY & DATE: ....

WHAT GUIDANCE IS THIS RUNE   HOW IM FEELING
GIVING ME TODAY?   ABOUT THIS DRAW?
                                    ☐ Happy
                                    ☐ Joyful
                                    ☐ Positive
                                    ☐ Energised
                                    ☐ Sad
Today's   ☐ Angry
Rune   ☐ Anguish
                                    ☐ Unhappy

DAY GRATEFUL FOR: MY FOCUS FOR TODAY:

How can today's rune help me make the most of today?

OD EVENING

AT FELT IN HARMONY TODAY?

                                    WAS MY ENERGY
                                    WELL SPENT
                                    TODAY?

AT FELT OUT OF BALANCE TODAY?
                                    ☐ Unfocused
                                    ☐ Distracted
                                    ☐ Steady
                                    ☐ Motivated
                                    ☐ Fully Engaged

W DID THE ENERGY OR MEANING OF TODAY'S RUNE REVEAL ITSELF?

hat small action I can take tomorrow to support my
ellbeing...

GOOD MORNING

DAY & DATE: _____

Today's Rune

WHAT GUIDANCE IS THIS RUNE GIVING ME TODAY?
_____
_____
_____
_____
_____
_____

HOW IM FEELING ABOUT THIS DAY
☐ Happy
☐ Joyful
☐ Positive
☐ Energised
☐ Sad
☐ Angry
☐ Anguish
☐ Unhappy

TODAY GRATEFUL FOR:
1. _____
2. _____
3. _____

MY FOCUS FOR TODAY:
_____
_____
_____

How can today's rune help me make the most of today

GOOD EVENING

WHAT FELT IN HARMONY TODAY?
_____
_____
_____

WHAT FELT OUT OF BALANCE TODAY?
_____
_____

WAS MY ENERGY WELL SPENT TODAY?
☐ Unfocused
☐ Distracted
☐ Steady
☐ Motivated
☐ Fully Engaged

HOW DID THE ENERGY OR MEANING OF TODAY'S RUNE REVEAL ITSELF
_____
_____

What small action I can take tomorrow to support my wellbeing...

THE RUNE IS A MIRROR; WHAT YOU SEE DEPENDS ON HOW YOU LOOK.

GOOD MORNING

DAY & DATE: ....

Today's Rune

WHAT GUIDANCE IS THIS RUNE GIVING ME TODAY?

_____
_____
_____
_____
_____

HOW IM FEELI ABOUT THIS DR
- ☐ Happy
- ☐ Joyful
- ☐ Positive
- ☐ Energised
- ☐ Sad
- ☐ Angry
- ☐ Anguish
- ☐ Unhappy

TODAY GRATEFUL FOR:

1. _____
2. _____
3. _____

MY FOCUS FOR TODAY:

_____
_____
_____

How can today's rune help me make the most of today

GOOD EVENING

WHAT FELT IN HARMONY TODAY?

_____
_____
_____

WHAT FELT OUT OF BALANCE TODAY?

_____
_____

WAS MY ENER WELL SPEN TODAY?
- ☐ Unfocused
- ☐ Distracted
- ☐ Steady
- ☐ Motivated
- ☐ Fully Engag

HOW DID THE ENERGY OR MEANING OF TODAY'S RUNE REVEAL ITSE

_____
_____

What small action I can take tomorrow to support m wellbeing...

OD MORNING

DAY & DATE: ....

Today's Rune

WHAT GUIDANCE IS THIS RUNE GIVING ME TODAY?

_____

_____

_____

_____

HOW IM FEELING ABOUT THIS DRAW?
- ☐ Happy
- ☐ Joyful
- ☐ Positive
- ☐ Energised
- ☐ Sad
- ☐ Angry
- ☐ Anguish
- ☐ Unhappy

DAY GRATEFUL FOR:

_____

_____

_____

MY FOCUS FOR TODAY:

_____

_____

_____

How can today's rune help me make the most of today?

OD EVENING

AT FELT IN HARMONY TODAY?

_____

_____

_____

AT FELT OUT OF BALANCE TODAY?

_____

_____

_____

WAS MY ENERGY WELL SPENT TODAY?
- ☐ Unfocused
- ☐ Distracted
- ☐ Steady
- ☐ Motivated
- ☐ Fully Engaged

W DID THE ENERGY OR MEANING OF TODAY'S RUNE REVEAL ITSELF?

_____

_____

hat small action I can take tomorrow to support my ellbeing…

GOOD MORNING

DAY & DATE: _____

Today's Rune

WHAT GUIDANCE IS THIS RUNE GIVING ME TODAY?

_____
_____
_____
_____
_____

HOW IM FEELING ABOUT THIS D...

- ☐ Happy
- ☐ Joyful
- ☐ Positive
- ☐ Energised
- ☐ Sad
- ☐ Angry
- ☐ Anguish
- ☐ Unhappy

TODAY GRATEFUL FOR:

1. _____
2. _____
3. _____

MY FOCUS FOR TODAY:

_____
_____
_____

How can today's rune help me make the most of today

GOOD EVENING

WHAT FELT IN HARMONY TODAY?

_____
_____
_____

WHAT FELT OUT OF BALANCE TODAY?

_____
_____
_____

WAS MY ENERGY WELL SPENT TODAY?

- ☐ Unfocused
- ☐ Distracted
- ☐ Steady
- ☐ Motivated
- ☐ Fully Engaged

HOW DID THE ENERGY OR MEANING OF TODAY'S RUNE REVEAL ITSE...

_____
_____

What small action I can take tomorrow to support m... wellbeing...

OD MORNING

DAY & DATE: _____

Today's Rune

WHAT GUIDANCE IS THIS RUNE GIVING ME TODAY?
_____
_____
_____
_____
_____

HOW IM FEELING ABOUT THIS DRAW?
☐ Happy
☐ Joyful
☐ Positive
☐ Energised
☐ Sad
☐ Angry
☐ Anguish
☐ Unhappy

DAY GRATEFUL FOR:
_____
_____
_____

MY FOCUS FOR TODAY:
_____
_____
_____

How can today's rune help me make the most of today?

OD EVENING

AT FELT IN HARMONY TODAY?
_____
_____
_____

AT FELT OUT OF BALANCE TODAY?
_____
_____

WAS MY ENERGY WELL SPENT TODAY?
☐ Unfocused
☐ Distracted
☐ Steady
☐ Motivated
☐ Fully Engaged

W DID THE ENERGY OR MEANING OF TODAY'S RUNE REVEAL ITSELF?
_____
_____

hat small action I can take tomorrow to support my ellbeing...

GOOD MORNING

DAY & DATE: _____

Today's Rune

WHAT GUIDANCE IS THIS RUNE GIVING ME TODAY?
_____
_____
_____
_____
_____

HOW IM FEELING ABOUT THIS DAY
- ☐ Happy
- ☐ Joyful
- ☐ Positive
- ☐ Energised
- ☐ Sad
- ☐ Angry
- ☐ Anguish
- ☐ Unhappy

TODAY GRATEFUL FOR:
1. _____
2. _____
3. _____

MY FOCUS FOR TODAY:
_____
_____
_____

How can today's rune help me make the most of today

GOOD EVENING

WHAT FELT IN HARMONY TODAY?
_____
_____
_____

WHAT FELT OUT OF BALANCE TODAY?
_____
_____
_____

WAS MY ENERGY WELL SPENT TODAY?
- ☐ Unfocused
- ☐ Distracted
- ☐ Steady
- ☐ Motivated
- ☐ Fully Engaged

HOW DID THE ENERGY OR MEANING OF TODAY'S RUNE REVEAL ITSELF
_____
_____

What small action I can take tomorrow to support my wellbeing...

GOOD MORNING   DAY & DATE: ....

Today's Rune

WHAT GUIDANCE IS THIS RUNE GIVING ME TODAY?

_____

_____

_____

_____

HOW IM FEELING ABOUT THIS DRAW?
- ☐ Happy
- ☐ Joyful
- ☐ Positive
- ☐ Energised
- ☐ Sad
- ☐ Angry
- ☐ Anguish
- ☐ Unhappy

TODAY GRATEFUL FOR:

_____

_____

_____

MY FOCUS FOR TODAY:

_____

_____

_____

> How can today's rune help me make the most of today?

GOOD EVENING

WHAT FELT IN HARMONY TODAY?

_____

_____

_____

WHAT FELT OUT OF BALANCE TODAY?

_____

_____

_____

WAS MY ENERGY WELL SPENT TODAY?
- ☐ Unfocused
- ☐ Distracted
- ☐ Steady
- ☐ Motivated
- ☐ Fully Engaged

HOW DID THE ENERGY OR MEANING OF TODAY'S RUNE REVEAL ITSELF?

_____

_____

> What small action I can take tomorrow to support my wellbeing…

GOOD MORNING

DAY & DATE: _____

Today's Rune

WHAT GUIDANCE IS THIS RUNE GIVING ME TODAY?
_____
_____
_____
_____
_____

HOW IM FEELI[NG] ABOUT THIS DR[AW]
- ☐ Happy
- ☐ Joyful
- ☐ Positive
- ☐ Energised
- ☐ Sad
- ☐ Angry
- ☐ Anguish
- ☐ Unhappy

TODAY GRATEFUL FOR:
1. _____
2. _____
3. _____

MY FOCUS FOR TODAY:
_____
_____
_____

How can today's rune help me make the most of today

GOOD EVENING

WHAT FELT IN HARMONY TODAY?
_____
_____
_____

WHAT FELT OUT OF BALANCE TODAY?
_____
_____
_____

WAS MY ENER[GY] WELL SPEN[T] TODAY?
- ☐ Unfocused
- ☐ Distracted
- ☐ Steady
- ☐ Motivated
- ☐ Fully Engag[ed]

HOW DID THE ENERGY OR MEANING OF TODAY'S RUNE REVEAL ITSE[LF]
_____
_____

What small action I can take tomorrow to support m[y] wellbeing…

"Mindfulness isn't about clearing your mind — it's about noticing what's already there."

GOOD MORNING

DAY & DATE: ....

Today's Rune

WHAT GUIDANCE IS THIS RUNE GIVING ME TODAY?

_____
_____
_____
_____
_____

HOW IM FEELING ABOUT THIS DAY

- ☐ Happy
- ☐ Joyful
- ☐ Positive
- ☐ Energised
- ☐ Sad
- ☐ Angry
- ☐ Anguish
- ☐ Unhappy

TODAY GRATEFUL FOR:

1. _____
2. _____
3. _____

MY FOCUS FOR TODAY:

_____
_____
_____

How can today's rune help me make the most of today

GOOD EVENING

WHAT FELT IN HARMONY TODAY?

_____
_____
_____

WHAT FELT OUT OF BALANCE TODAY?

_____
_____
_____

WAS MY ENERGY WELL SPENT TODAY?

- ☐ Unfocused
- ☐ Distracted
- ☐ Steady
- ☐ Motivated
- ☐ Fully Engaged

HOW DID THE ENERGY OR MEANING OF TODAY'S RUNE REVEAL ITSELF

_____
_____

What small action I can take tomorrow to support my wellbeing...

GOOD MORNING   DAY & DATE: _____

Today's Rune

WHAT GUIDANCE IS THIS RUNE GIVING ME TODAY?
_____
_____
_____
_____
_____

HOW IM FEELING ABOUT THIS DRAW?
☐ Happy
☐ Joyful
☐ Positive
☐ Energised
☐ Sad
☐ Angry
☐ Anguish
☐ Unhappy

TODAY GRATEFUL FOR:
_____
_____

MY FOCUS FOR TODAY:
_____
_____

How can today's rune help me make the most of today?

GOOD EVENING

WHAT FELT IN HARMONY TODAY?
_____
_____
_____

WHAT FELT OUT OF BALANCE TODAY?
_____
_____

WAS MY ENERGY WELL SPENT TODAY?
☐ Unfocused
☐ Distracted
☐ Steady
☐ Motivated
☐ Fully Engaged

HOW DID THE ENERGY OR MEANING OF TODAY'S RUNE REVEAL ITSELF?
_____
_____

What small action I can take tomorrow to support my wellbeing...

GOOD MORNING

DAY & DATE: _____

Today's Rune

WHAT GUIDANCE IS THIS RUNE GIVING ME TODAY?

_____
_____
_____
_____

HOW IM FEELING ABOUT THIS DAY

☐ Happy
☐ Joyful
☐ Positive
☐ Energised
☐ Sad
☐ Angry
☐ Anguish
☐ Unhappy

TODAY GRATEFUL FOR:

1. _____
2. _____
3. _____

MY FOCUS FOR TODAY:

_____
_____
_____

How can today's rune help me make the most of today

GOOD EVENING

WHAT FELT IN HARMONY TODAY?

_____
_____
_____

WAS MY ENERGY WELL SPENT TODAY?

☐ Unfocused
☐ Distracted
☐ Steady
☐ Motivated
☐ Fully Engaged

WHAT FELT OUT OF BALANCE TODAY?

_____
_____
_____

HOW DID THE ENERGY OR MEANING OF TODAY'S RUNE REVEAL ITSELF

_____
_____

What small action I can take tomorrow to support my wellbeing…

GOOD MORNING

DAY & DATE: ....

Today's Rune

WHAT GUIDANCE IS THIS RUNE GIVING ME TODAY?

_____

_____

_____

_____

HOW IM FEELING ABOUT THIS DRAW?
- ☐ Happy
- ☐ Joyful
- ☐ Positive
- ☐ Energised
- ☐ Sad
- ☐ Angry
- ☐ Anguish
- ☐ Unhappy

TODAY GRATEFUL FOR:

_____

_____

_____

MY FOCUS FOR TODAY:

_____

_____

_____

How can today's rune help me make the most of today?

GOOD EVENING

WHAT FELT IN HARMONY TODAY?

_____

_____

_____

WHAT FELT OUT OF BALANCE TODAY?

_____

_____

_____

WAS MY ENERGY WELL SPENT TODAY?
- ☐ Unfocused
- ☐ Distracted
- ☐ Steady
- ☐ Motivated
- ☐ Fully Engaged

HOW DID THE ENERGY OR MEANING OF TODAY'S RUNE REVEAL ITSELF?

_____

_____

What small action I can take tomorrow to support my wellbeing...

GOOD MORNING

DAY & DATE: _____

Today's Rune

WHAT GUIDANCE IS THIS RUNE GIVING ME TODAY?

_____
_____
_____
_____
_____
_____

HOW IM FEELI ABOUT THIS DE
- ☐ Happy
- ☐ Joyful
- ☐ Positive
- ☐ Energised
- ☐ Sad
- ☐ Angry
- ☐ Anguish
- ☐ Unhappy

TODAY GRATEFUL FOR:

1. _____
2. _____
3. _____

MY FOCUS FOR TODAY:

_____
_____
_____

How can today's rune help me make the most of today

GOOD EVENING

WHAT FELT IN HARMONY TODAY?

_____
_____
_____

WHAT FELT OUT OF BALANCE TODAY?

_____
_____
_____

WAS MY ENER WELL SPEN TODAY?
- ☐ Unfocused
- ☐ Distracted
- ☐ Steady
- ☐ Motivated
- ☐ Fully Engag

HOW DID THE ENERGY OR MEANING OF TODAY'S RUNE REVEAL ITSE

_____
_____

What small action I can take tomorrow to support m wellbeing...

GOOD MORNING   DAY & DATE: _____

Today's Rune

WHAT GUIDANCE IS THIS RUNE GIVING ME TODAY?
_____
_____
_____
_____

HOW IM FEELING ABOUT THIS DRAW?
☐ Happy
☐ Joyful
☐ Positive
☐ Energised
☐ Sad
☐ Angry
☐ Anguish
☐ Unhappy

TODAY GRATEFUL FOR:
_____
_____
_____

MY FOCUS FOR TODAY:
_____
_____
_____

How can today's rune help me make the most of today?

GOOD EVENING

WHAT FELT IN HARMONY TODAY?
_____
_____
_____

WHAT FELT OUT OF BALANCE TODAY?
_____
_____
_____

WAS MY ENERGY WELL SPENT TODAY?
☐ Unfocused
☐ Distracted
☐ Steady
☐ Motivated
☐ Fully Engaged

HOW DID THE ENERGY OR MEANING OF TODAY'S RUNE REVEAL ITSELF?
_____
_____

What small action I can take tomorrow to support my wellbeing…

GOOD MORNING

DAY & DATE: ....

Today's Rune

WHAT GUIDANCE IS THIS RUNE GIVING ME TODAY?

_____
_____
_____
_____
_____

HOW IM FEELI[NG] ABOUT THIS D[AY]
- ☐ Happy
- ☐ Joyful
- ☐ Positive
- ☐ Energised
- ☐ Sad
- ☐ Angry
- ☐ Anguish
- ☐ Unhappy

TODAY GRATEFUL FOR:

1. _____
2. _____
3. _____

MY FOCUS FOR TODAY:

_____
_____
_____

How can today's rune help me make the most of today

GOOD EVENING

WHAT FELT IN HARMONY TODAY?

_____
_____
_____

WHAT FELT OUT OF BALANCE TODAY?

_____
_____

WAS MY ENER[GY] WELL SPEN[T] TODAY?
- ☐ Unfocused
- ☐ Distracted
- ☐ Steady
- ☐ Motivated
- ☐ Fully Engag[ed]

HOW DID THE ENERGY OR MEANING OF TODAY'S RUNE REVEAL ITSE[LF]

_____
_____

What small action I can take tomorrow to support m[y] wellbeing...

Every rune drawn is a conversation. Sometimes with the world, sometimes with yourself.

GOOD MORNING

DAY & DATE: _____

Today's Rune

WHAT GUIDANCE IS THIS RUNE GIVING ME TODAY?

_____
_____
_____
_____
_____

HOW IM FEELI ABOUT THIS D

- ☐ Happy
- ☐ Joyful
- ☐ Positive
- ☐ Energise
- ☐ Sad
- ☐ Angry
- ☐ Anguish
- ☐ Unhappy

TODAY GRATEFUL FOR:

1. _____
2. _____
3. _____

MY FOCUS FOR TODAY:

_____
_____
_____

How can today's rune help me make the most of today

GOOD EVENING

WHAT FELT IN HARMONY TODAY?

_____
_____
_____

WHAT FELT OUT OF BALANCE TODAY?

_____
_____
_____

WAS MY ENE WELL SPEN TODAY?

- ☐ Unfocused
- ☐ Distracted
- ☐ Steady
- ☐ Motivated
- ☐ Fully Engag

HOW DID THE ENERGY OR MEANING OF TODAY'S RUNE REVEAL ITSE

_____
_____

What small action I can take tomorrow to support m wellbeing...

GOOD MORNING

DAY & DATE: ....

WHAT GUIDANCE IS THIS RUNE GIVING ME TODAY?

_____

_____

_____

_____

Today's Rune

HOW IM FEELING ABOUT THIS DRAW?
☐ Happy
☐ Joyful
☐ Positive
☐ Energised
☐ Sad
☐ Angry
☐ Anguish
☐ Unhappy

TODAY GRATEFUL FOR:

_____

_____

_____

MY FOCUS FOR TODAY:

_____

_____

_____

How can today's rune help me make the most of today?

GOOD EVENING

WHAT FELT IN HARMONY TODAY?

_____

_____

_____

WHAT FELT OUT OF BALANCE TODAY?

_____

_____

WAS MY ENERGY WELL SPENT TODAY?
☐ Unfocused
☐ Distracted
☐ Steady
☐ Motivated
☐ Fully Engaged

HOW DID THE ENERGY OR MEANING OF TODAY'S RUNE REVEAL ITSELF?

_____

_____

What small action I can take tomorrow to support my wellbeing...

GOOD MORNING

DAY & DATE: _____

Today's Rune

WHAT GUIDANCE IS THIS RUNE GIVING ME TODAY?
_____
_____
_____
_____
_____

HOW IM FEELI[NG] ABOUT THIS DR[AW]
- ☐ Happy
- ☐ Joyful
- ☐ Positive
- ☐ Energised
- ☐ Sad
- ☐ Angry
- ☐ Anguish
- ☐ Unhappy

TODAY GRATEFUL FOR:
1. _____
2. _____
3. _____

MY FOCUS FOR TODAY:
_____
_____
_____

How can today's rune help me make the most of today

GOOD EVENING

WHAT FELT IN HARMONY TODAY?
_____
_____
_____

WHAT FELT OUT OF BALANCE TODAY?
_____
_____
_____

WAS MY ENER[GY] WELL SPEN[T] TODAY?
- ☐ Unfocused
- ☐ Distracted
- ☐ Steady
- ☐ Motivated
- ☐ Fully Engag[ed]

HOW DID THE ENERGY OR MEANING OF TODAY'S RUNE REVEAL ITSE[LF]
_____
_____

What small action I can take tomorrow to support m[y] wellbeing…

GOOD MORNING

DAY & DATE: _____

WHAT GUIDANCE IS THIS RUNE GIVING ME TODAY?

_____
_____
_____
_____

Today's Rune

HOW IM FEELING ABOUT THIS DRAW?

☐ Happy
☐ Joyful
☐ Positive
☐ Energised
☐ Sad
☐ Angry
☐ Anguish
☐ Unhappy

TODAY GRATEFUL FOR:

_____
_____
_____

MY FOCUS FOR TODAY:

_____
_____
_____

How can today's rune help me make the most of today?

GOOD EVENING

WHAT FELT IN HARMONY TODAY?

_____
_____
_____

WHAT FELT OUT OF BALANCE TODAY?

_____
_____
_____

WAS MY ENERGY WELL SPENT TODAY?

☐ Unfocused
☐ Distracted
☐ Steady
☐ Motivated
☐ Fully Engaged

HOW DID THE ENERGY OR MEANING OF TODAY'S RUNE REVEAL ITSELF?

_____
_____

What small action I can take tomorrow to support my wellbeing...

GOOD MORNING

DAY & DATE: _____

Today's Rune

WHAT GUIDANCE IS THIS RUNE GIVING ME TODAY?

_____
_____
_____
_____
_____

HOW IM FEELI[NG] ABOUT THIS D[AY]
- ☐ Happy
- ☐ Joyful
- ☐ Positive
- ☐ Energised
- ☐ Sad
- ☐ Angry
- ☐ Anguish
- ☐ Unhappy

TODAY GRATEFUL FOR:

1. _____
2. _____
3. _____

MY FOCUS FOR TODAY:

_____
_____
_____

How can today's rune help me make the most of today

GOOD EVENING

WHAT FELT IN HARMONY TODAY?

_____
_____
_____

WHAT FELT OUT OF BALANCE TODAY?

_____
_____
_____

WAS MY ENER[GY] WELL SPEN[T] TODAY?
- ☐ Unfocused
- ☐ Distracted
- ☐ Steady
- ☐ Motivated
- ☐ Fully Engag[ed]

HOW DID THE ENERGY OR MEANING OF TODAY'S RUNE REVEAL ITSE[LF]

_____
_____

What small action I can take tomorrow to support m[y] wellbeing...

OD MORNING DAY & DATE: ....

WHAT GUIDANCE IS THIS RUNE GIVING ME TODAY?

_____

_____

_____

_____

Today's Rune

HOW IM FEELING ABOUT THIS DRAW?
- ☐ Happy
- ☐ Joyful
- ☐ Positive
- ☐ Energised
- ☐ Sad
- ☐ Angry
- ☐ Anguish
- ☐ Unhappy

DAY GRATEFUL FOR:

_____

_____

_____

MY FOCUS FOR TODAY:

_____

_____

_____

How can today's rune help me make the most of today?

OD EVENING

AT FELT IN HARMONY TODAY?

_____

_____

HAT FELT OUT OF BALANCE TODAY?

_____

_____

WAS MY ENERGY WELL SPENT TODAY?
- ☐ Unfocused
- ☐ Distracted
- ☐ Steady
- ☐ Motivated
- ☐ Fully Engaged

W DID THE ENERGY OR MEANING OF TODAY'S RUNE REVEAL ITSELF?

_____

_____

hat small action I can take tomorrow to support my ellbeing...

GOOD MORNING

DAY & DATE: _____

Today's Rune

WHAT GUIDANCE IS THIS RUNE GIVING ME TODAY?
_____
_____
_____
_____
_____

HOW IM FEELING ABOUT THIS DAY
- ☐ Happy
- ☐ Joyful
- ☐ Positive
- ☐ Energised
- ☐ Sad
- ☐ Angry
- ☐ Anguish
- ☐ Unhappy

TODAY GRATEFUL FOR:
1. _____
2. _____
3. _____

MY FOCUS FOR TODAY:
_____
_____
_____

How can today's rune help me make the most of today

GOOD EVENING

WHAT FELT IN HARMONY TODAY?
_____
_____
_____

WHAT FELT OUT OF BALANCE TODAY?
_____
_____
_____

WAS MY ENERGY WELL SPENT TODAY?
- ☐ Unfocused
- ☐ Distracted
- ☐ Steady
- ☐ Motivated
- ☐ Fully Engaged

HOW DID THE ENERGY OR MEANING OF TODAY'S RUNE REVEAL ITSELF
_____
_____

What small action I can take tomorrow to support my wellbeing...

**FROM STONE
AND STORY,
THE RUNES SPEAK
AND WE LISTEN.**

GOOD MORNING

DAY & DATE: ....

Today's Rune

WHAT GUIDANCE IS THIS RUNE GIVING ME TODAY?

_____
_____
_____
_____
_____

HOW IM FEELI ABOUT THIS D
- ☐ Happy
- ☐ Joyful
- ☐ Positive
- ☐ Energised
- ☐ Sad
- ☐ Angry
- ☐ Anguish
- ☐ Unhappy

TODAY GRATEFUL FOR:

1. _____
2. _____
3. _____

MY FOCUS FOR TODAY:

_____
_____
_____

How can today's rune help me make the most of today

GOOD EVENING

WHAT FELT IN HARMONY TODAY?

_____
_____
_____

WHAT FELT OUT OF BALANCE TODAY?

_____
_____
_____

WAS MY ENER WELL SPEN TODAY?
- ☐ Unfocused
- ☐ Distracted
- ☐ Steady
- ☐ Motivated
- ☐ Fully Engag

HOW DID THE ENERGY OR MEANING OF TODAY'S RUNE REVEAL ITSE

_____
_____

What small action I can take tomorrow to support m wellbeing…

OD MORNING   DAY & DATE: ....

WHAT GUIDANCE IS THIS RUNE GIVING ME TODAY?

_____

_____

_____

_____

Today's Rune

HOW IM FEELING ABOUT THIS DRAW?
- ☐ Happy
- ☐ Joyful
- ☐ Positive
- ☐ Energised
- ☐ Sad
- ☐ Angry
- ☐ Anguish
- ☐ Unhappy

DAY GRATEFUL FOR:

_____

_____

_____

MY FOCUS FOR TODAY:

_____

_____

_____

How can today's rune help me make the most of today?

OD EVENING

AT FELT IN HARMONY TODAY?

_____

_____

_____

AT FELT OUT OF BALANCE TODAY?

_____

_____

_____

WAS MY ENERGY WELL SPENT TODAY?
- ☐ Unfocused
- ☐ Distracted
- ☐ Steady
- ☐ Motivated
- ☐ Fully Engaged

W DID THE ENERGY OR MEANING OF TODAY'S RUNE REVEAL ITSELF?

_____

_____

What small action I can take tomorrow to support my ellbeing…

GOOD MORNING

DAY & DATE: _____

Today's Rune

WHAT GUIDANCE IS THIS RUNE GIVING ME TODAY?

_____
_____
_____
_____
_____

HOW IM FEELI[NG] ABOUT THIS D[AY]
- ☐ Happy
- ☐ Joyful
- ☐ Positive
- ☐ Energise[d]
- ☐ Sad
- ☐ Angry
- ☐ Anguish
- ☐ Unhappy

TODAY GRATEFUL FOR:

1. _____
2. _____
3. _____

MY FOCUS FOR TODAY:

_____
_____
_____

How can today's rune help me make the most of today

GOOD EVENING

WHAT FELT IN HARMONY TODAY?

_____
_____
_____

WHAT FELT OUT OF BALANCE TODAY?

_____
_____

WAS MY ENER[GY] WELL SPEN[T] TODAY?
- ☐ Unfocused
- ☐ Distracted
- ☐ Steady
- ☐ Motivated
- ☐ Fully Engag[ed]

HOW DID THE ENERGY OR MEANING OF TODAY'S RUNE REVEAL ITSE[LF]

_____
_____

What small action I can take tomorrow to support m[y] wellbeing...

Weekly Check-Ins

WEEK BEGINNING: ....

WHY THIS RUNE? (CHOSEN OR DRAWN AT RANDOM?
_____
_____

Rune of the Week

WHAT'S THE FIRST THOUGHT OR FEELING THIS RUNE SPARKS FOR ME?
_____
_____
_____

What is one practical action I can take this week to embody this rune's energy?

WHAT WERE THE MOST SIGNIFICANT EVENTS, EMOTIONS, OR CHALLENGES OF MY WEEK?
_____
_____
_____

HOW WELL DID MY ACTIONS AND CHOICES ALIGN WITH THE INTENTIONS I SET?
_____
_____
_____

WAS MY ENERGY WELL SPENT THIS WEEK?
☐ Unfocused
☐ Distracted
☐ Steady
☐ Motivated
☐ Fully Engaged

WHAT INSIGHTS OR LESSONS EMERGED FROM THIS WEEK'S EXPERIENCES?
_____
_____
_____

What will I carry forward, adjust, or release as I step into the next week?

WEEK BEGINNING: ....

WHY THIS RUNE? (CHOSEN OR DRAWN AT RANDOM

_____

_____

Rune of the Week

WHAT'S THE FIRST THOUGHT OR FEELING THIS RUNE SPARKS FOR ME?

_____

_____

_____

What is one practical action I can take this week to embody this rune's energy?

WHAT WERE THE MOST SIGNIFICANT EVENTS, EMOTIONS, OR CHALLENGES OF MY WEEK? _____

_____

_____

HOW WELL DID MY ACTIONS AND CHOICES ALIGN WITH THE INTENTIONS I SET?

_____

_____

_____

WHAT INSIGHTS OR LESSONS EMERGED FROM THIS WEEK'S EXPERIENCES?

_____

_____

_____

WAS MY ENE[RGY]
WELL SPEN[T]
THIS WEE[K]

- ☐ Unfocused
- ☐ Distracted
- ☐ Steady
- ☐ Motivated
- ☐ Fully Enga[ged]

What will I carry forward, adjust, or release as I step into the next week?

WEEK BEGINNING: ....

WHY THIS RUNE? (CHOSEN OR DRAWN AT RANDOM?)

Rune of the Week

WHAT'S THE FIRST THOUGHT OR FEELING THIS RUNE SPARKS FOR ME?

What is one practical action I can take this week to embody this rune's energy?

WHAT WERE THE MOST SIGNIFICANT EVENTS, EMOTIONS, OR CHALLENGES OF MY WEEK?

HOW WELL DID MY ACTIONS AND CHOICES ALIGN WITH THE INTENTIONS I SET?

WHAT INSIGHTS OR LESSONS EMERGED FROM THIS WEEK'S EXPERIENCES?

WAS MY ENERGY WELL SPENT THIS WEEK?

☐ Unfocused
☐ Distracted
☐ Steady
☐ Motivated
☐ Fully Engaged

What will I carry forward, adjust, or release as I step into the next week?

WEEK BEGINNING: ....

WHY THIS RUNE? (CHOSEN OR DRAWN AT RANDOM)
_____
_____

Rune of the Week

WHAT'S THE FIRST THOUGHT OR FEELING THIS RUNE SPARKS FOR ME?
_____
_____
_____

What is one practical action I can take this week to embody this rune's energy?

WHAT WERE THE MOST SIGNIFICANT EVENTS, EMOTIONS, OR CHALLENGES OF MY WEEK?
_____
_____
_____

HOW WELL DID MY ACTIONS AND CHOICES ALIGN WITH THE INTENTIONS I SET?
_____
_____
_____

WAS MY ENERGY WELL SPENT THIS WEEK?

☐ Unfocused
☐ Distracted
☐ Steady
☐ Motivated
☐ Fully Engaged

WHAT INSIGHTS OR LESSONS EMERGED FROM THIS WEEK'S EXPERIENCES?
_____
_____
_____

What will I carry forward, adjust, or release as I step into the next week?

WEEK BEGINNING: ....

WHY THIS RUNE? (CHOSEN OR DRAWN AT RANDOM?)
_____
_____

Rune of the Week

WHAT'S THE FIRST THOUGHT OR FEELING THIS RUNE SPARKS FOR ME?
_____
_____
_____

What is one practical action I can take this week to embody this rune's energy?

WHAT WERE THE MOST SIGNIFICANT EVENTS, EMOTIONS, OR CHALLENGES OF MY WEEK? _____
_____
_____

HOW WELL DID MY ACTIONS AND CHOICES ALIGN WITH THE INTENTIONS I SET?
_____
_____

WAS MY ENERGY WELL SPENT THIS WEEK?
☐ Unfocused
☐ Distracted
☐ Steady
☐ Motivated
☐ Fully Engaged

WHAT INSIGHTS OR LESSONS EMERGED FROM THIS WEEK'S EXPERIENCES?
_____
_____
_____

What will I carry forward, adjust, or release as I step into the next week?

WEEK BEGINNING: ....

WHY THIS RUNE? (CHOSEN OR DRAWN AT RANDOM)

Rune of the Week

WHAT'S THE FIRST THOUGHT OR FEELING THIS RUNE SPARKS FOR ME?

What is one practical action I can take this week to embody this rune's energy?

WHAT WERE THE MOST SIGNIFICANT EVENTS, EMOTIONS, OR CHALLENGES OF MY WEEK?

HOW WELL DID MY ACTIONS AND CHOICES ALIGN WITH THE INTENTIONS I SET?

WHAT INSIGHTS OR LESSONS EMERGED FROM THIS WEEK'S EXPERIENCES?

WAS MY ENERGY WELL SPENT THIS WEEK

☐ Unfocused
☐ Distracted
☐ Steady
☐ Motivated
☐ Fully Engaged

What will I carry forward, adjust, or release as I step into the next week?

WEEK BEGINNING: ....

WHY THIS RUNE? (CHOSEN OR DRAWN AT RANDOM?)
_____
_____

Rune of
the Week

WHAT'S THE FIRST THOUGHT OR FEELING THIS RUNE SPARKS FOR ME?
_____
_____
_____

What is one practical action I can take this week to embody this rune's energy?
_____
_____
_____

WHAT WERE THE MOST SIGNIFICANT EVENTS, EMOTIONS, OR CHALLENGES OF MY WEEK?
_____
_____
_____

HOW WELL DID MY ACTIONS AND CHOICES ALIGN WITH THE INTENTIONS I SET?
_____
_____
_____

WAS MY ENERGY WELL SPENT THIS WEEK?

☐ Unfocused
☐ Distracted
☐ Steady
☐ Motivated
☐ Fully Engaged

WHAT INSIGHTS OR LESSONS EMERGED FROM THIS WEEK'S EXPERIENCES?
_____
_____
_____

What will I carry forward, adjust, or release as I step into the next week?
_____
_____

WEEK BEGINNING: ....

WHY THIS RUNE? (CHOSEN OR DRAWN AT RANDOM)
_____
_____

Rune of the Week

WHAT'S THE FIRST THOUGHT OR FEELING THIS RUNE SPARKS FOR ME?
_____
_____
_____

What is one practical action I can take this week to embody this rune's energy?

WHAT WERE THE MOST SIGNIFICANT EVENTS, EMOTIONS, OR CHALLENGES OF MY WEEK?
_____
_____
_____

HOW WELL DID MY ACTIONS AND CHOICES ALIGN WITH THE INTENTIONS I SET?
_____
_____
_____

WHAT INSIGHTS OR LESSONS EMERGED FROM THIS WEEK'S EXPERIENCES?
_____
_____
_____

WAS MY ENERGY WELL SPENT THIS WEEK

☐ Unfocused
☐ Distracted
☐ Steady
☐ Motivated
☐ Fully Engaged

What will I carry forward, adjust, or release as I step into the next week?

WEEK BEGINNING: ....

WHY THIS RUNE? (CHOSEN OR DRAWN AT RANDOM?)

_____

_____

WHAT'S THE FIRST THOUGHT OR FEELING THIS RUNE SPARKS FOR ME?

_____

_____

_____

Rune of the Week

What is one practical action I can take this week to embody this rune's energy?

_____

_____

WHAT WERE THE MOST SIGNIFICANT EVENTS, EMOTIONS, OR CHALLENGES OF MY WEEK?

_____

_____

HOW WELL DID MY ACTIONS AND CHOICES ALIGN WITH THE INTENTIONS I SET?

_____

_____

WAS MY ENERGY WELL SPENT THIS WEEK?

☐ Unfocused
☐ Distracted
☐ Steady
☐ Motivated
☐ Fully Engaged

WHAT INSIGHTS OR LESSONS EMERGED FROM THIS WEEK'S EXPERIENCES?

_____

_____

What will I carry forward, adjust, or release as I step into the next week?

_____

WEEK BEGINNING: _____

WHY THIS RUNE? (CHOSEN OR DRAWN AT RANDOM)

_____
_____

Rune of the Week

WHAT'S THE FIRST THOUGHT OR FEELING THIS RUNE SPARKS FOR ME?

_____
_____

What is one practical action I can take this week to embody this rune's energy?

_____

WHAT WERE THE MOST SIGNIFICANT EVENTS, EMOTIONS, OR CHALLENGES OF MY WEEK?

_____
_____

HOW WELL DID MY ACTIONS AND CHOICES ALIGN WITH THE INTENTIONS I SET?

_____
_____

WHAT INSIGHTS OR LESSONS EMERGED FROM THIS WEEK'S EXPERIENCES?

_____
_____

WAS MY ENERGY WELL SPENT THIS WEEK?

☐ Unfocused
☐ Distracted
☐ Steady
☐ Motivated
☐ Fully Engaged

What will I carry forward, adjust, or release as I step into the next week?

_____

WEEK BEGINNING: _____

WHY THIS RUNE? (CHOSEN OR DRAWN AT RANDOM?)
_____
_____

Rune of
the Week

WHAT'S THE FIRST THOUGHT OR FEELING THIS
RUNE SPARKS FOR ME?
_____
_____
_____

What is one practical action I can take this week to
embody this rune's energy?

WHAT WERE THE MOST SIGNIFICANT EVENTS, EMOTIONS, OR
CHALLENGES OF MY WEEK? _____
_____
_____

HOW WELL DID MY ACTIONS AND CHOICES ALIGN
WITH THE INTENTIONS I SET?
_____
_____
_____

WAS MY ENERGY
WELL SPENT
THIS WEEK?

☐ Unfocused
☐ Distracted
☐ Steady
☐ Motivated
☐ Fully Engaged

WHAT INSIGHTS OR LESSONS EMERGED FROM
THIS WEEK'S EXPERIENCES?
_____
_____
_____

What will I carry forward, adjust, or release as I step
into the next week?

WEEK BEGINNING: ....

WHY THIS RUNE? (CHOSEN OR DRAWN AT RANDOM)

_____

_____

Rune of the Week

WHAT'S THE FIRST THOUGHT OR FEELING THIS RUNE SPARKS FOR ME?

_____

_____

What is one practical action I can take this week to embody this rune's energy?

WHAT WERE THE MOST SIGNIFICANT EVENTS, EMOTIONS, OR CHALLENGES OF MY WEEK?

_____

_____

HOW WELL DID MY ACTIONS AND CHOICES ALIGN WITH THE INTENTIONS I SET?

_____

_____

_____

WHAT INSIGHTS OR LESSONS EMERGED FROM THIS WEEK'S EXPERIENCES?

_____

_____

WAS MY ENERGY WELL SPENT THIS WEEK?

☐ Unfocused
☐ Distracted
☐ Steady
☐ Motivated
☐ Fully Engaged

What will I carry forward, adjust, or release as I step into the next week?

Monthly Tracker - Overview & Reflections

Month _____

Monthly Rune Draw Tracker

Record your daily rune draws and notice the patterns and insights that emerge.

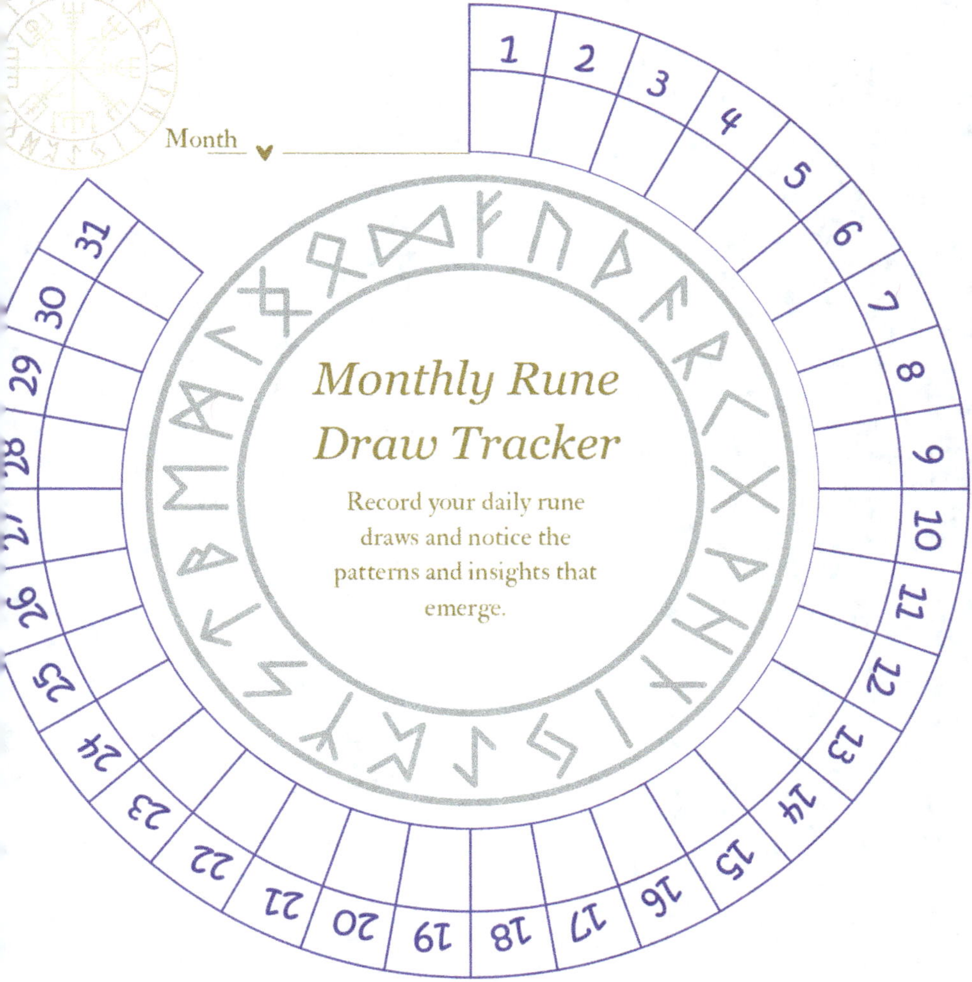

What themes, repeated messages, or patterns have you noted in how each rune shows up in your life.

Month ♥ _____

Monthly Rune Draw Tracker

Record your daily rune draws and notice the patterns and insights that emerge.

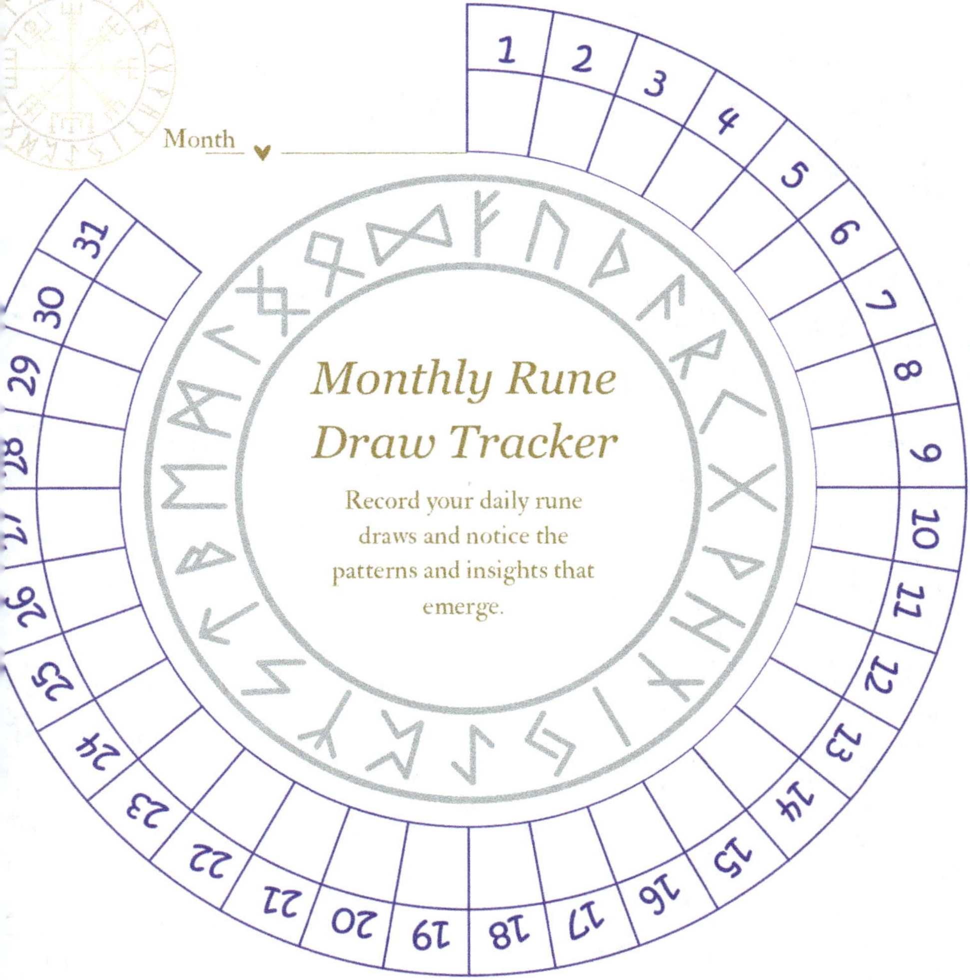

What themes, repeated messages, or patterns have you noted in how each rune shows up in your life.

Month _____

Monthly Rune Draw Tracker

Record your daily rune draws and notice the patterns and insights that emerge.

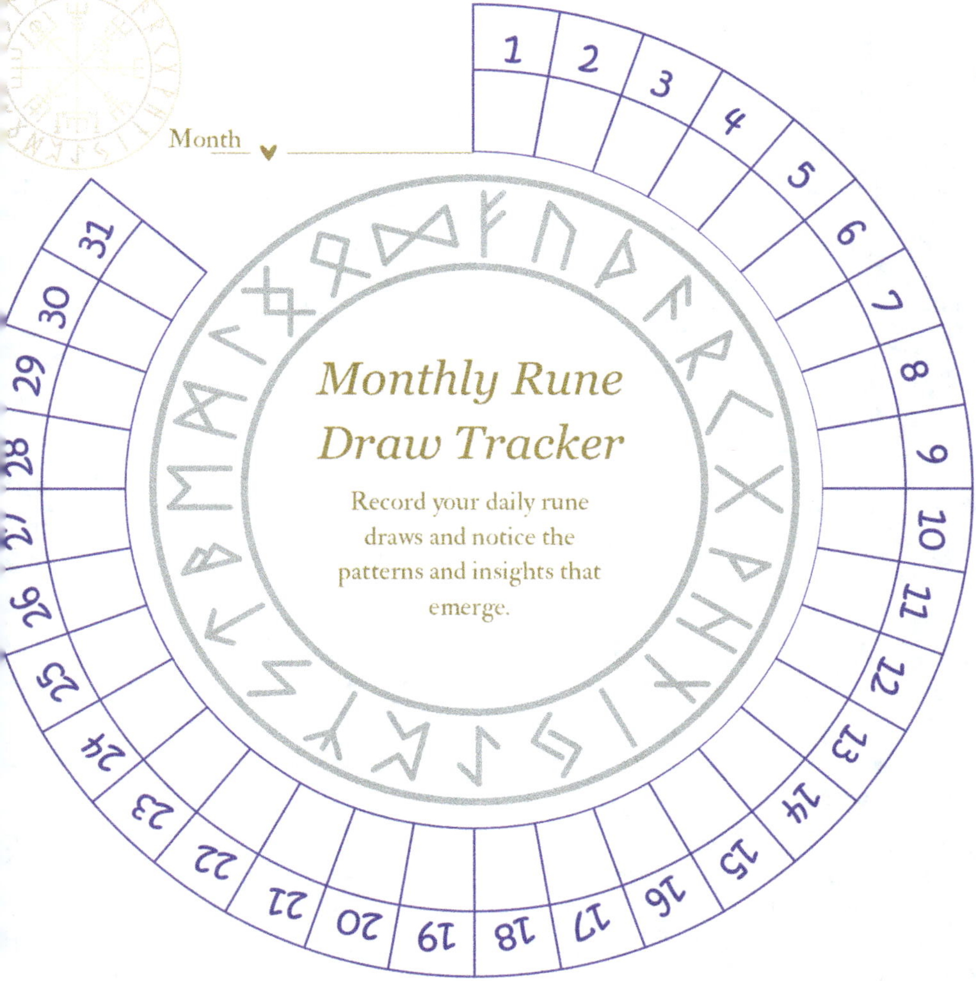

What themes, repeated messages, or patterns have you noted in how each rune shows up in your life.

Blank Rune Outlines

"DECORATE, COLOUR, OR WRITE WITHIN AND AROUND THIS RUNE. LET YOUR MIND WANDER. CAPTURE WHAT THIS SYMBOL MEANS TO YOU TODAY."

ANSUZ – WISDOM AND COMMUNICATION
THEME: DIVINE MESSAGE, EXPRESSION, INSPIRATION

GEBO – GIFT AND CONNECTION
THEME: GENEROSITY, BALANCE, PARTNERSHIP

ALGIZ – SACRED PROTECTION
THEME: DEFENCE, BOUNDARIES, DIVINE CONNECTION

LAGUZ – FLOW AND INTUITION
THEME: WATER, EMOTION, INNER KNOWING

ODIN'S RUNE – THE SACRED UNKNOWN
(AKA WYRD OR BLANK RUNE)
THEME: TRUST, FATE, DIVINE WILL

www.ingramcontent.com/pod-product-compliance
Lightning Source LLC
Chambersburg PA
CBHW071242070526
44583CB00017B/2288